Geo Cruikshank

MR PUNCH.

Etched by George Cruikshank.

PUNCH AND JUDY
A Short History with the Original Dialogue

John Payne Collier

Illustrated by
George Cruikshank

Foreword by
Tony Sarg

Bibliographical Note by
Anne Lyon Haight

DOVER PUBLICATIONS, INC.
Mineola, New York

Bibliographical Note

This Dover edition, first published in 2006, is an unabridged republication of the work published in 1929 in a limited edition of 376 copies by Rimington & Hooper, New York, under the title *Punch and Judy, Accompanied by the Dialogue of the Puppet-Show, An Account of Its Origin, and of Puppet-Plays in England.* This ISSUE NUMBER TWO of the Savoy Editions was originally designed and printed by D. B. Updike, The Merrymount Press, Boston. (The first edition was published in 1828 by S. Prowett, London.)

A facsimile of George Cruikshank's signature appears on the first page of the Dover reprint, as it did in the 1929 edition. While the pagination has been slightly altered for this reprint, nothing from the original work has been omitted.

Library of Congress Cataloging-in-Publication Data

Punch and Judy.
  Punch and Judy : a short history with the original dialogue / John Payne Collier ; illustrated by George Cruikshank ; foreword by Tony Sarg ; bibliographical note by Anne Lyon Haight.
    p. cm.
  Originally published: New York : Rimington & Hooper, 1929.
  ISBN 0-486-44903-3 (pbk.)
  1. Punch and Judy. I. Collier, John Payne, 1789–1883. II. Cruikshank, George, 1792–1878. III. Title.

PN1979.P9 2006
791.5'3—dc22

2006046283

Manufactured in the United States of America
Dover Publications, Inc., 31 East 2nd Street, Mineola, N.Y. 11501

CONTENTS

FOREWORD

THE Tragical Comedy of Punch and Judy, as presented in these pages, follows a version of the puppet-play set down more than a century ago, and even then hoary with age. George Cruikshank's inimitable drawings are as inseparably a part of the "Punch" tradition as the Tenniel illustrations are of "Alice in Wonderland."

And what a play it is! What an unexampled category of crime! Mr. Punch, himself, that braggart, blusterer, wife-beater, strutting Don Juan, with a half dozen murders to his credit, what a very prince of villains he is! Truly, children were fed upon strong meat in the days that were. In these anæmic times, the career of this arch-scoundrel of the puppet-stage strikes a full and robust note. Those were the days when rogues were rogues; and when children, untroubled by educational theories or parental scruples, were permitted to rejoice naturally in the cracking of heads, the din of battle, the triumph of Unworthiness over Virtue and the Law.

Something primitive within ourselves, deep buried in the subconscious, takes delight in this sly and consistent rogue, this jubilant and ruthless scapegrace, Mr. Punch, and is more glad when he cheats the hangman and turns the tables on the Devil than if he had paid the just penalty of his crimes. It is this want of virtue within ourselves—even the most moral of us, I fancy—which has made the naughty fellow what he is.

There is something infinitely fascinating about those relics of the far-distant past which still live and breathe in our own times, their survival through the centuries the best evidence of their vitality. The pack of cards, for instance: what a sense it gives one of forgotten pomps and glories, moving wraithlike behind the pictured faces of King and Queen and Knave. Or the flower ceremonies of Easter, relic of the ancient pagan festival of Spring. Or the humble barber-pole, the red and blue of its stripes symbolizing the arterial and the venous blood, the white the winding bandage—what a tale it could tell of mediæval days when surgeon and barber were the same individual and it was set up before the physician's house as the sign of his profession! These and many another bit of the past still live in our own day, although we have long ago forgotten their origin and significance.

So, also, survives the Punch and Judy Show—if, indeed, motion pictures have not backed it off the boards altogether in the last decade.

Its hero, Punch, as well as the traditional characters of the Italian puppet-show with whom he was associated for some hundreds of years before he met his wife, Judy, or had a play of his own—Harlequin, Brighella, Pantaloon, Scaramouch, and all the motley company which made up the personnel of the Commedia del Arte—all of these characters are proudly ancient, tracing back their lineage, it is believed, to the burlesque actors of ancient Rome.

"It was a matter of course," says the *Encyclopædia Britannica*, "that remnants of the ancient popular dramatic entertainments should have survived in particular abundance on Italian soil. They were to be recognized in the improvised farces performed at the courts, in the churches, and among the people; the Roman carnival had preserved its wagon-plays, and various links remained to connect the modern comic drama of the Italians with the Atellanes and mimes of their ancestors."

During the Fifteenth and Sixteenth Centuries, the popular character comedy, relic of the ancient Roman farces, took on a new lease of life and manifested itself in double form. The *Improvised Comedy*, known as the Commedia del Arte, consisted of scenes unwritten save in skeleton, and played by professional actors who improvised their own lines; and, distinct from this growth, the *Masked Comedy* developed, the action of which was carried out by typical figures wearing masks and speaking in local dialects, but without improvisation.

From the Commedia del Arte and the Masked Comedy the traditional characters, themselves perhaps derived from the burlesque actors of ancient Rome—Pulcinella, Harlequin, Brighella, and the lot —were transferred to the puppet-show, borrowing costume, type, and rôles from the living actors for the glorification of the marionette stage.

To trace the exploits of even one of the heroes of the legendary puppet drama—Mr. Punch, for instance—would require a lifetime of research. The casual student may only lightly touch upon a few of the highlights of his long and checkered career.

There are various theories about the origin of this beloved rogue.

"Punch," says *The Century Dictionary*, "is the descendant of the clown, or Pulcinella, of the Neapolitan comedy; the part is thought to have been created by Silvio Fiorillo, a comedian, about 1600."

"Early in the Eighteenth Century," says Madge Anderson in her book, *Heroes of the Puppet Stage*, "antiquarians excavating near Herculaneum found a little statue of an actor with a nose just like Pulcinella's, and a nut cracker chin like his, and two humps and a fat stomach. It is supposed to be a portrait of Maccus, one of the Roman mimes. The mimes were mimics, who were fond of making fun of everyone and, especially, of caricaturing other actors' plays. They even attempted tragedy and turned it to farce with their nonsense. Maccus was one of the Atellan players, a company of actors who came from their native town of Atella and went about giving their comic plays on high wooden trestles. Atella was in the neighbourhood of Herculaneum and Pompeii, where Maccus' portraits were found, and not far from Naples, the headquarters of Pulcinella. Maccus spoke the Oscan dialect, the language of the neighbourhood where Pulcinella learned his dialect, and he may have been the great-great-grandfather of Mr. Punch.

"This ancient jester was witty and insolent. He could not endure to be contradicted and his chief argument was a cudgel; first he knocked his opponents down and then he reasoned with them. He loved to imitate the cries of birds, especially the cackle of a hen, with his pivetta. This was a little whistle that the Atellan players used when they caricatured the metallic sound of the tragic actors' voices speaking through their great masks. The Punch and Judy showman still cries Punch's Root-to-too-it through a mouth-piece like the whistle Maccus used in Rome."

An old Neapolitan legend ascribes another origin for the fascinating Mr. Punch. It says that, in vintage time, a company of strolling players came to Acerra, near Naples, when the country folk were celebrating the grape harvest, and were so taken with the comical appearance and rustic wit of one of the grape-gatherers, the village hump-back, a fellow with a huge nose, whose name was Puccio d'Aniello, that they persuaded him to join their company.

This Puccio d'Aniello became a great favourite, for nobody could keep from laughing at his antics; and when he died, another actor put on a false nose and a hump on his back and took, also, the name, Puccio d'Aniello—a name which, in time, became slurred by soft Italian voices into "Pulcinella."

What one may do, others may follow, and soon there were a host of chicken-breasted, hump-backed clowns in the Italian cities, all cracking jokes and polls interchangeably, all playing the buffoon to a delighted populace, and all bearing the name Pulcinella. So popular was this character that a host of marionette Pulcinellas soon took possession of the puppet-stage.

This seems a probable explanation of the birth of our hero, although there are those who cling to the idea that the name, Pulcinella, since it means "little chicken," was given to the character because of his crowing-cry, his beak-nose, and chicken-breast.

So, indeed, might Charlie Chaplin serve as proto-type for a traditional figure. A score of living imitators might arise, wearing his dress, playing his parts; and a marionette made in his image, playing a definite range of characters, might hand on to generations yet unborn the personality of that great comedian.

In the course of time, Pulcinella, now wholly relegated to the puppet-stage, carried by travelling showmen from one country to another, spread from Italy to the whole of mediæval Europe, equally favoured by populace and nobles, his crude horse-play as successful in France, Germany, England, as in his native Italy. Become cosmopolitan, he proceeded to take to himself a variety of names. In England he became Punchinello, shortened presently to Punch; in France, he was known as Polichinelle; in Germany, Kasperle; in Turkey, Karaguez, or "Black Eye."

During the Middle Ages, Punch enjoyed great liberty of action, appearing in religious drama, political satire, and even opera; entertaining the company at noblemen's palaces—in many of which were well-equipped puppet-stages—as well as in his humbler function as actor in a travelling marionette troupe, playing on the streets, or as chief attraction at the fairs.

"In Catholic countries"—I quote again from
Madge Anderson—"the puppets retained the respect of the public as long as they kept their religious connections. But as soon as they ventured out-
side the church, they adopted worldly manners and
morals and the clergy began to think that the wooden
actors were too irreverent to appear in the churches.
The puppets could not always be depended upon to
behave. They mixed too many humourous dialogues,
parodies, popular songs, and dances with the Bible
stories. Although the clergy cast them off, still the
puppets were usually free from religious persecution.
When the English Puritans waged a bitter war
against the degenerate drama of their time, they ig-
nored the offenses of Mr. Punch, and when the German church placed a ban on the stage and all players were classed as vagabonds and law-breakers, the
puppets were considered beneath the notice of the
religious authorities. So the wooden Thespians seized
the playhouses and took the place of the outcast actors. The living players became puppet-showmen and
delivered the lines for the doll actors so feelingly and
managed their gestures so intelligently that the

marionettes captured the hearts of the German people. It was the puppets who carried the flickering torch of the German drama through the dark days of the Thirty Years' War and all the misery that followed. In France and England the little actors never commanded such respect as they received in Germany, where, during the age of Shakespeare and Molière, there was no real literature but hymns, and no drama except that of the marionettes."

Although Punch appeared during his early days as fellow-actor with Harlequin, Brighella, Pantaloon, and other traditional characters, in the course of time an epic, which excluded his associates, grew up in England about his own personality. He acquired a wife and child and a dog Toby—and fell afoul of the Law and the Devil. Only Scaramouch, of all his ancient comrades, continued to figure in the lurid tale of his misdeeds.

Gradually this epic crystallized; and, wherever the showman set up his booth, the children of Merrie England, both young and old, gathered open-mouthed at the shrill note of Punch's trumpet, on street-corners, or at the fairs, to rejoice in the Simon-pure wickedness of their hero ; wickedness magnificently untinged by promptings of conscience or remorse.

Punch was Punch—bad as they make 'em. And how they loved him throughout the centuries!

Although the play of Punch must have varied, according to the talents of the showman, it was, in essentials, that which is printed in this book.

Once, in my childhood, I saw the redoubtable hero in his gilded booth, and carried away an impression of ancientness, of a vast and shadowy background, which, being a child, I was unable to put into words. There he strutted, Punch the immortal, untarnished, unchanged. There he crowed his braggart songs, wielded his club, thwacked heads royally, murdered his wife and child and the policeman, and threw them out of the window; and there he hanged the hangman with the noose intended for his own neck, and beat the Devil to death with his cudgel. "Huzza! Huzza! The Devil is dead!" A deliciously unregenerate ending, a veritable triumph of roguery!

It was a great show, satisfying. And I think with sorrow that he who overcame the powers of darkness so gloriously is perhaps himself about to become the victim of the powers of light. Is Punch indeed immortal, or has mortality at last laid hold upon him? Are the movies driving the lusty rogue into his grave, after his long centuries of merry sins? I can only hope not.

TONY SARG

New York, May 15, 1929

PUNCH AND JUDY
A Short History with
the Original Dialogue

INTRODUCTION.

WITH the assistance of our friend, Mr. GEORGE CRUIKSHANK, we are about to fill up a *hiatus* in theatrical history.

It is singular, that, to the present day, no attempt has been made to illustrate the origin, biography, and character of a person so distinguished and notorious as Mr. PUNCH. His name and his performances are familiar to all ranks and ages; yet nobody has hitherto taken the trouble, in this country or abroad, to make any inquiries regarding himself, his family, or connections. The "studious Bayle" is recorded to have repeatedly sallied from his retreat, at the sound of the cracked trumpet, announcing his arrival in Rotterdam; and we ourselves, who have often hunted our favourite performer from street to street, saw the late Mr. Windham, then one of the Secretaries of State, on his way from Downing Street to the House of Commons, on a night of important debate, pause like a truant boy, until the whole performance was concluded, to enjoy a hearty laugh at the whimsicalities of "the motley hero." But it is needless to particularise :—Punch has

> "make our youth to laugh,
> Until they scarcely could look on for tears;"

while the old have stood by, "delighted with delight" of others, and themselves, too, enjoying the ludicrous representation. Why the interest has hitherto been limited to the period of representation, and whether it has not in part arisen from inability to satisfy it, is not for us to explain. We confine ourselves to an endeavour, in some degree, to supply the deficiency.

The contrast between the neglect Mr. Punch has experienced, and the industry employed in collecting particulars relating to other performers of far less reputation, is remarkable. If an actor, on any of our public stages, attain only a moderate degree of eminence, hundreds are on the alert to glean the minutest particulars of his "birth, parentage, and education, life, character, and behaviour;" and thousands look out for them with eagerness in all the newspapers and periodicals of the day. Punch has never been *famæ petitor:*

"That last distemper of the sober brain," *

as Marvell calls it, has never been one of his weaknesses; but, nevertheless, it is undeniable, that his fame has spread, "without his stirring," over all

---

* How this unhappy thought has run the gauntlet of authorship from the time of Simplicius (Comm. ad Epict. xlviii.) Διο χαι εσχατος, λεγετχι των παθων, &c. Tacitus has it thus; *Etiam sapientibus cupido gloriæ novissima exuitur.* (Hist. Lib. iv.) Montaigne places the love of glory among the *humeurs desraisonnables* of men, and adds, *Les philosophes mêmes se defacent plus tard, et plus envis, de cette-cy que de nulle autre.* (*Essays*, L. i. c. 41.) Ben Jonson says the same thing:
"Ambition—is the last affection
A high mind can put off."—(*Catiline*, Act iii. Sc. 2.)
It is also found in Massinger:
"'Though desire of fame be the last weakness
Wise men put off."—(*Very Woman*, Act v. Sc. 4.)
And Owen Feltham follows Tacitus very closely: "Desire of glory is the last garment that even wise men lay aside."—(*Resolves*, xv.)
We may wind up the whole with Milton, who, like others,

the kingdoms of the civilized world. To use the
wordy periphrasis of Dr. Johnson,

> " Let observation, with extensive view,
>   Survey mankind from China to Peru ; "

if it can, and it will every where behold Punch dis-
pensing " the luxury of a laugh." It is literally
true, that, some years ago, he found his way to Can-
ton ; and that, since the South American Revolution,
he has been seen even on the western side of the
Andes. He is, perhaps, himself in part to blame for
the neglect we have noticed. Several of the principal supporters of our theatres, in our own day, have
given their memoirs to the world, either by writing
them with their own hands, or by furnishing the
materials to others ; and the works of this kind by
dead actors, " the forgotten of the stage," consist
of many volumes. Whether it has arisen from an
absence of that vanity (may we call it ?) which has

---

has deemed the thought common property, when he tells us
in *Lycidas,* that fame is

>   " That last infirmity of noble mind : "

upon which, in fact, Marvell's line, above quoted (and which
is to be found in his " Satire on Flecno, an English priest, at
Rome ") is only a parody.

at times influenced his histrionic rivals, or from a somewhat haughty reluctance, on his part, to gratify public curiosity, we know not; but whatever injury it may do the sale of our volume, it ought not in fairness to be concealed, that, towards us, the object and subject of the appended inquiry has preserved an obstinate silence which, in any other individual, we should say amounted to incivility. Even when informed that his portrait was to be drawn by Mr. George Cruikshank, it did not at all change his deportment. This circumstance is certainly to be regretted; but we flatter ourselves that our own unaided resources have furnished much curious and interesting information : and if, by its publication, we give offence, we must "aby the event," knowing that, as Mr. Punch was deaf to our request, he will not listen to our apology.

Another remark may not here be out of its place : Poetry is unquestionably out of fashion; and because it was not "set by," as perhaps it ought to have been, the greatest (in every sense of the word) author of our day turned his attention to a different and more popular mode of writing. His astonishing success induced others to follow his example : they, too, tried their hands at historical novels; but,

wanting the genius of their original, they endeavoured to keep up the interest of their narratives by the
introduction of biographical matter. Still they
found they were not read, and their next step was to
make the dead the means of satirising and censuring
the living; until, in a short time, this thin disguise
was thrown aside, and novels became the vehicles of
private anecdotes and malicious disclosures. Such
is now the characteristic of our literature, excepting
in as far as it is corrected by the "Colossus" afore-
said; and we appeal to all the puffs in all the
papers within the last four or five years, for the
proof, that fashionable slander, and the exposure of
secret intrigues of persons in high life, have been
made the chief recommendation and attraction of
such productions. The course has been, to assign
the work of a "scribbling garreteer" to some Lord
or Lady of distinguished connections, and to represent, that, for the sake of gratifying a mania for the
consumption of pen, ink, and paper, he or she has
condescended, first to play the spy, and afterwards
the traitor, to friends and acquaintances.

Nothing of this kind will be found in the volume
now in the reader's hand; and although the biography of the Punch family is, necessarily, partially

included in our plan, those who expect that we shall detail particulars of his private amours and failings will be disappointed. Ariosto tells such as may not like certain parts of his gay poem, to turn over so many of its leaves:* we advise those, who feel vexation at the preceding statement, to shut our book altogether; or, at least, not to do more than cast their eyes upon the plates: since they know by whom the drawings were made, it would, perhaps, be too much to suppose they could consent to relinquish that gratification. Those incidents of his life which our hero has chosen to make known, are of course not omitted; but, in our details and observations, we have spoken of him only in his public capacity,—as an actor of first-rate talents and of the most extensive celebrity.

---

* See the introductory stanzas to Book xxviii. of the *Orlando Furioso*.

> *Lasciate questo canto, che senz' esso,*
> *Può star l'istoria, &c.*

CHAPTER I.

ORIGIN OF PUNCH IN ITALY.

Mr. Punch (whose original family name was probably *Pulcinella*) first came into existence at Acerra,
an ancient city at a short distance from Naples. The
date of this event is differently stated by authors who
have incidently mentioned him; Riccoboni* fixing it
before the year 1600, and Gimma† and Signorelli‡

---

* He uses general terms, and his authority is not much to
be relied on : *Histoire du Théatre Italien depuis la Decadence de
la Comedie Latine, &c.*

† *Italia Letterata,* vol. i. p. 196.

‡ *Storia Critica de' Teatri antiche e moderne.* —Nap. 1777. It
is to be observed, however, that the Dottore Pietro Napoli
Signorelli relies for his assertion on the statement of Gimma
in his *Italia Letterata.* As one proof that Pulcinella was not

after the commencement of the seventeenth century. The words of Gimma are very precise, and as he enters into particulars, it seems safe to rely upon his authority for this important fact: he says, " Silvio Fiorillo, comedian, who procured himself to be call- ed the Captain Matamoros, invented the Neapolitan Pulcinella; to which Andrea Calcese, who had the sur- name of Ciuccio, by study and natural grace added much. Calcese was a tailor, and died in the plague of the year 1656: he imitated the peasants of Acerra, a very ancient city of Terra di Lavoro, not far from Naples." Signorelli expressly calls Punch, *un buffone* * *dell' Acerra;* and of the Neapolitans in general, he re- marks (p. 231) that, " from a certain national vivacity and disposition, they have been at all times distin-

known before the year 1600, it may be noticed that he is not mentioned by one of the burlesque poets of Italy, who flour- ished anterior to that date, *Berni, Molza, Casa, Lasca, &c.*

* Voltaire, in his *Questions sur L'Encyclopedie,* thus speaks of the etymology of the Italian word *buffone,* after ridiculing the classical derivation pedantically assigned to it — "Ce mot de *bufon* est reçu depuis longtems chez les Italiens et chez les Espagnols: il signifiait *mimus, scurra, joculator,* mime, farceur, jongleur. Ménage, après Saumaise, le dérive de *bocca infiata,* boursouflé; et en effet on veut dans un boufon un visage rond et la joue rebondie. Les Italiens disent *bufo magro,* maigre boufon, pour exprimer un mauvois plaisant qui ne vous fait pas rire."

guished for their talent in imitating the ridiculous on their stages." * Hence more than one of the amusing personages in their impromptu comedies, or *commedie à soggetto,* inserted by Riccoboni among the plates attached to his work, have had their origin in that lively and luxurious capital. †

In order to give a notion of the species of dramatic entertainment in which these various characters, and among them Pulcinella, were engaged, a further short quotation from Signorelli's work will be useful : he is referring to the state of the Italian comedy in the beginning of the seventeenth century. "In gen-

---

* Rapin, in his "Reflexions on Modern Poetry," says of the Italians generally, that they are *naturellement comediens,* and that they *expriment mieux le ridicule des choses,* adding that their language was well adapted to the purpose.

† They are the ancient and modern Harlequin—the ancient and modern Pantaloon — the ancient and modern Doctor — Beltrame di Milano—Scapin—the Italian Captain—the Spanish Captain—the Neapolitan Scaramouche — Calabrian Giangurgolo—Mezzettin—Tartaglia—the Neapolitan Pulcinella, and Narcisin of Malabergo. In another of his productions, Riccoboni speaks very contemptuously of the *impromptu* comedy, observing that it *ne merite pas un si beau nom, et que l on devroit plûtôt appeller Farce.* He afterward calls it *ancienne et mercenaire,* and tells us that it succeeded *la comedie Latine; foible et immodeste dans son origine, mais plus chaste et plus ingenieuse dans la suite. "Reflexions Historiques et Critiques,"* &c. *8vo. Par.* 1738.

eral (he says), the public comedians travelled over Italy, representing certain theatrical performances, called comedies of *art*, in contradistinction to comedies of *learning*, recited in the academies and in private dwellings by well-bred actors for their pleasure and exercise. The plan or plot of the fables, they call it, *à soggetto*, was noted down, as well as the substance and distribution of each scene, while the dialogue was left to the will of the representers. Such histrionic farces contained various trivial buffooneries, and different masks were employed in them."

These performances, in which the actor was left to his own talents and discretion in furnishing the dialogue, were once extremely popular throughout Italy; but from the very nature of the representation, it unluckily happens, that not a single specimen has been handed down to our time. The few sentences extracted above, we think, will serve to explain a good deal of the supposed mystery of those ancient English "plots," or "platforms" of theatrical representations discovered in Dulwich College; in which the celebrated Tarlton and others were concerned, and which so long puzzled Malone, Steevens, and some of the other commentators on Shakspeare.* Several of the most distinguished actors of that day

* See Malone's Shakspeare, by Boswell, iii. 256, &c.

had travelled in Italy, and were remarkable for their *impromptu;* and Nash, who had been there, in one of his tracts especially terms the famous clown, Kempe, a "Harlequin" (a character constantly engaged in such representations), and adds that his fame had extended south of the Alps.*

However, to pursue this topic would lead us away from the object of our present inquiry. We take it for granted, that Silvio Fiorillo invented Pulcinella, and first introduced him as a variety in the list of buf- foons required to represent the impromptu comedies of Naples: but, although he may date his separate existence from about the year 1600, it is a matter of much doubt, whether he was not, in fact, only a branch of a family of far greater antiquity. The discovery, in the year 1727, of a bronze statue of a mime, called by the Romans *Maccus,* has indeed led some antiqua- ries to the conclusion, that he was, in fact, Pulcinella under a different name, but with the same attributes, and among them a hump-back and a large nose. †

But that the figure was meant for *Maccus* at all seems mere speculation, and that Pulcinella and *Maccus* had any thing in common, but hump and nose, is at least

---

* See the Dedication of his "Almond for a Parrot," printed about the year 1598.

† See D'Israeli's "Curiosities of Literature," iii. 9.

as questionable. The Vice, as he was called, of the ancient Moralities was common, we apprehend, to the early theatrical representations of most countries: his business was to relieve the weightier part of the performance by his ridiculous actions, jests, and buffooneries. He was unquestionably the original of the Clown, or Fool, of the old English Drama; and we think the conjecture is at least plausible, that he was the original also of Harlequin,* and his near relative Pulcinella. The chief appendage of the Vice was a gilt wooden sword, and this also belonged to the old Clown, or Fool, not only in England, but abroad. Rabelais, speaking of certain presents made by Panurge to the fool Triboullet, says; *Panurge à sa venue luy donna une vessie de porc, bien enflée et resonnante, à cause des poys qui dedans estoient: plus, une espée de boys bien dorée: plus, une petite gibessiere faicte d'une coque de tortue:†* which we thus translate for the benefit of such as may not understand the antiquated French,—"Panurge, on his arrival, gave him a pig's bladder well inflated, and resounding by reason of the peas that were within it: moreover, a

---

* Riccoboni, *Histoire du Theatre Italien*, quotes several authorities, to shew that a Mime like Harlequin was known to the ancients: he relies chiefly on an expression of Apuleius, *Mimi centunculo*, with reference to the patch-work dress.

† Chap. 42, edit. 1553.

wooden sword well gilt: moreover, a small pouch, made of a shell of a tortoise." Those who consult Mr. Douce's "Illustrations," and particularly his essay on the "Clowns and Fools of Shakspeare," will find that the bladder at the end of a stick, the gilt wooden sword,* and the pouch or budget, formed part of the equipments of that personage in this country. The wooden sword directly connects Harlequin with the ancient Vice, and more modern Fool,† although we have now enjoined him to silence, and have converted the instrument, with which of old he cudgelled the Devil, into a talisman to raise him.

The dress, too, of Harlequin corresponds very much with the *motley* or parti-coloured habit of the clowns of our old dramatic poets. It is true, that the different

---

* If this coincidence had occurred to Mr. D'Israeli, he would not have said (Cur. Lit. iii. 10, note) that "the light lath-sword of Harlequin had hitherto baffled his most painful researches."

† In Spain he is called the *Gracioso,* and his dress and equipments are nearly the same as they were in England : the morris-bells and the bladders are particularly mentioned by Cervantes, in his description of the Parliament of Death : "whilst they were thus discoursing, it fell out, that one of the company came toward them, clad for *the Fool* in the play, with morris-bells, and at the end of a stick he had three cows' bladders full blown," &c. Shelton's *Don Quixote,* part ii. ch. xi.

hues have been arranged with greater regularity, and
the patches are of smaller size. The ordinary habili-
ments of Punch at the present day, preserved by ancient usage, with his pointed fool's-cap, bear a much
nearer resemblance ; and this is one circumstance
that evidences the strong family-resemblance between
the Vice, Harlequin, and Pulcinella.* Riccoboni represents the *ancient* Harlequin in a dress composed of
patches, as if his ragged clothes had been often mend-
ed, and Goldoni speaks of him as originally a poor
foolish dolt. There can be little doubt that this was
the real origin of the *motley* of the dramatic and
domestic fools in former times. They were retained,
or were supposed to be retained, by the nobility, commonly out of charity, and one of their ordinary appel-
lations was *Patch.* Cardinal Wolsey had a fool whose
parental name has been lost, and he is now only known
by the nick-name belonging to his profession.

Upon the continent, to this day, Harlequin is as talk-
ative as ever, even if his jokes are a little less coarse,
and his satire kept within narrower bounds. Voltaire,
in his *Encyclopedie* † and elsewhere, quotes several

* Dr. Johnson, in a note on "Hamlet" (Act iii. Scene 4), as-
serts positively, that " the modern Punch is descended from
the ancient Vice ;" but this opinion is disputed by Mr. Douce,
" Illustrations of Shakspeare," ii. 251.

† Vol. iv. p. 427, edit. 1775.

capital sayings and aphorisms by Harlequin; but the account that Addison gives of him would hardly lead us to suppose that in his time he possessed so much wit and acuteness. He tells us that, in Italy, " Harlequin's part is made up of blunders and absurdities : he is to mistake one name for another, to forget his errands, to stumble over queens, and to run his head against every post that comes in his way. This is all attended with something so comical in the voice and gestures, that a man who is sensible of the folly of the part can hardly forbear to be pleased with it." * Much of this character has been transferred to the clowns of our pantomimes, since Harlequin was elevated in station and degraded in understanding. †

---

* Travels, p. 77, edit. 1718.

† A good deal has been written on the etymology of the word Harlequin : it is very clear that the fanciful derivations from Francis the First's ridicule of *Charles Quint,* and from M. de *Harlay-quint,* in the reign of Henry III. of France, are unfounded. The Rev. Mr. Todd quotes a letter of M. Raulin, dated 1521, which affords clear evidence that the "*familiam Harlequini*" was even then " *antiquam;*" and as early as the time of Odericus Vitalis, A. D. 1143, the same family is mentioned as the *familia Herlechini.* This decisive authority for its high antiquity was not known to Mr. Todd. Whether *Harlequinus,* or *Herlechinus,* were really the name of any family, or whether it was a corruption of the old French *arlot,* a cheat,

Concluding, then, that Punch is one of the *familia Harlequini*, and that their common parent was the Vice of the old Moralities, the question arises, to what circumstance he owes the deformity of his figure, and why his nose, by its length, is rendered so obtrusive a feature? We can only answer, that it pleased his inventor, Silvio Fiorillo, to make him so; and, perhaps, he did it in some degree with a view of rendering him more ridiculous, and to distinguish him more effectually from other characters of not dissimilar habits and propensities in the *impromptu* comedies: hence too, probably, the peculiar quality of his voice, to which Addison alludes. One striking characteristic of Punch is his amorous inclination; and it is generally supposed that individuals with the personal defect for which he is remarkable, are peculiarly "given to the feminines;" and the Italian proverb relating to the length of nose needs not, if it could, be repeated. Among Riccoboni's plates is one of Giangurgolo of Calabria, and he is represented with a much larger nose than that of Pulcinella.* In the time of Shakspeare, it seems to

must still, and perhaps will ever, remain a matter of dispute among the learned.

* And with some reason, if we confide in the statement of Voltaire in his *Encycl.* Art. *Bouc.*

have been the custom for usurers on the stage to wear large false noses; but, perhaps, it was intended thus to indicate that they were generally of the Jewish persuasion.*

According to Quadrio, in his *Storia d'ogni Poesia,* the name of our hero has relation to the length of his nose: he would spell it Pullicinello from *Pulliceno,* which Mr. D'Israeli translates "turkey-cock," in allusion to the beak of that bird. Baretti has it Pulcinella, because that word in Italian means a hen-chicken, whose cry the voice of Punch is said to resemble. — Pollicenello, as it has also been written, in its etymology from *pollice,* "the thumb," goes upon the mistaken presumption that his size was always diminutive, like that of our English worthy, of cow-swallowing memory. The French *Ponche* has been fancifully derived from no less a personage than Pontius Pilate of the old Mysteries, whom, in barbarous times, the Christians wished to abuse and ridicule.† If we cannot settle the disputed point, it is very evident that in future ingenuity and learning will be thrown away in attempting further elucidation.

At what time and in what country Punch became a

* See note 21 to the "Jew of Malta," in *Dodsley's Old Plays,* new edition, vol. viii. p. 279. Also vol. xii. p. 396.

† Some have supposed that the English name of Punch was

mere puppet as well as a living performer, we have
no distinct information; but it is to be inferred, perhaps, that the transmigration first took place in the
land of his birth, and after his popularity had been
fully established.* The pleasure derived by the lower
orders from his performances might lead to the imitation of his manners and actions in little: in the same
way, as will be hereafter seen, that the most applauded
representations of our own stage, in the reigns of
Elizabeth and James, were very soon made the subjects
of "motions" or puppet-plays. One man could thus,
by a little ingenuity, and at a very cheap rate, repre-

a corruption of *paunch,* from the large protuberance in front
with which this personage is provided. This is alluded to by
Tom Brown, in his "Common Place Book," where he is ad-
verting to Dunton's *Athenians.* "As for their skill in etymology (he says — vol. iii. p. 283, edit. 1744), I shall instance in
two, viz., *surplice,* from *super* and *plico;* and *Punch,* quasi
paunch," &c.

* He was a puppet in France at an early date; and, in 1721,
Le Sage wrote pieces to be represented by Pulcinella and his
wooden coadjutors. Le Sage had previously produced dramas
for the *Theatre de la Foire,* which being silenced in 1721, he and
Francisque, his *co-laborateur,* procured puppets instead of living actors. Piron ridiculed their dullness, and, in a piece
called *Arlequin Deucalion,* introduced Punch laughing, and
apparently with some justice, at the want of wit in Le Sage's
representations.

sent half a dozen or more characters, and the delusion was aided by the peculiar voice given to Punch by artificial means. Ere long he became the hero of the exhibition; and other characters, such as Harlequin and Scaramouch, by degrees sunk into insignificance. The last, as well as the Doctor, is still preserved in some of the performances in this country, and we are assured by those who have recently travelled, that the Spanish Captain, the Calabrian with a huge nose, and some others of the personages enumerated by Riccoboni, yet figure in the Italian puppet-shows. In Holland, about ten years ago, we were present at one of the performances of Punch (there usually called *Tooneelgek*, "stage-fool" or "buffoon"), in which a number of other characters peculiar to the country, and among them a burgomaster and a Friesland peasant, were introduced.*

* In Germany he is commonly known by the name of *Hanns Wurst* among the lower orders; the literal translation of which is our Jack Pudding, *Hanns* being John or Jack, and *Wurst* a pudding or sausage. He is also called *Polischinel*, and *Hanns Wurst*, used as a generic term for any kind of buffoon.

CHAPTER II.

ORIGIN AND PROGRESS OF PUPPET-PLAYS
IN ENGLAND.

BEFORE we proceed farther, it will be necessary to
consider, briefly, the antiquity and nature of puppet-
plays in this country. It is the more proper to do
so, because they form a branch of our drama which
has never been examined by the historians of our
stage with as much interest and industry as the subject deserves. When we mention that no less a man
than Dr. Johnson was of opinion, that puppets were
so capable of representing even the plays of Shakspeare, that Macbeth might be performed by them
as well as by living actors; * it will be evident, from
such a fact only, that the inquiry is far from unim-
portant. In connection with this opinion, and con-

---

* See Malone's Shakspeare by Boswell, xi. p. 301.

firmatory of it, we may add, that a person of the name of Henry Rowe, shortly before the year 1797, did actually, by wooden figures, for a series of years, go through the action of the whole of that tragedy, while he himself repeated the dialogue which belongs to each of the characters.*

Puppet-plays are of very ancient date in England; and, if they were not contemporary with our Mysteries, they probably immediately succeeded them. There is reason to think that they were coeval, at least, with our Moralities; and, in Catholic times, it is not a very

* He was also called the York Trumpeter, having been born in that city, and having "blown a battle blast" at Culloden. He was born in 1726, and after the rebellion he retired to his native place; where, for about fifty years, he graced with his instrument the entrance of the Judges twice a year into York. He was a very well known character, and for a long time before his death in 1800 was master of a puppet-show. In 1797, he published his edition of Macbeth, with new notes and various emendations. At his decease, the following lines, never yet printed, were written upon him:

" When the great Angel blows the judgment trump,
  He also must give Harry Rowe a thump:
  If not, poor Harry never will awake,
  But think it is his own trumpet, by mistake.
  He blew it all his life, with greatest skill,
  And but for want of breath had blown it still."

violent supposition to conclude that the Priests themselves made use even of the images of the Saints and
Martyrs, perhaps, for this very purpose : it is well
ascertained, not only that they did not scruple to employ the churches, but that those sacred edifices were
considered the fittest places for our earliest dramatic
representations.*

"Motion" is the most general term by which they
are mentioned by our ancient authors, and especially
by our dramatists : thus Shakspeare, in the *Winter's
Tale* (Act iv. Scene 2), makes Autolycus say : "Then
he compassed a *motion* of the Prodigal Son, and married a tinker's wife within a mile of where my land
and living lies." It would be easy to multiply quotations to the same point from nearly all his contemporaries, but one is as good as a thousand. The
nature and one method of their representation at that
period, and doubtless long before, may be seen at the
close of Ben Jonson's *Bartholomew Fair*. He there
makes Lanthern Leatherhead convert the story of
Hero and Leander (then very popular from Marlow's
and Chapman's translation, or rather paraphrase of it)
into a "motion" or puppet-play; and he combines
with it the well known friendship of Damon and Py-

* See the new edition of *Dodley's Old Plays*, vol. i. p. xliii.
et seq.

thias, a story long before dramatised. The exhibitor, standing above and working the figures, "interprets" for them, and delivers the burlesque dialogue he supposes to pass between the characters. In the same Poet's *Tale of a Tub* (Act v.), In-and-in Medley presents a "motion" for the amusement of the company, connecting it with the plot of the comedy itself. Here he explains the scenes as he proceeds, something in the manner of the ancient Dumb-Shews before the different acts of *Ferrex and Porrex*, the *Misfortunes of Arthur*, and other old tragedies,* but the puppets are not represented as speaking among themselves. Ben Jonson may always be relied on in matters relating to the customs and amusements of our ancestors, as he was a very minute observer of them; and from his evidence, we may infer, that there were, at least, two varieties in the puppet-plays of his time, — one with the dialogue, as in *Bartholomew Fair;* and the other without it, but

* These dumb-shews have been thought peculiar to our elder stage on the first rise of tragedy; but R. Brome employs the same expedient of conveying information on the progress of the story in his *Queen and Concubine*, which was printed in 1659. During the progress of it, a supernatural character, called "a genius," explains what is passing, much in the same way as the owner of "a motion" interpreted for his figures.

with a descriptive accompaniment, as in the *Tale of a Tub.**

It is evident, from many passages in our old writers that might be adduced if necessary, that "motions" were very popular with the lower orders: they frequently rivalled and imitated the performers on the regular stages. Hence, perhaps, a portion of the abuse with which they were commonly assailed by some of our dramatic poets, who were, of course, anxious to bring them as much as possible into contempt. It is established, on the authority of Dekker, and other pamphleteers and play-writers of about the same period, that the subjects of the "villainous motions" were often borrowed from the most successful dramatic entertainments. Shakspeare's *Julius Cæsar* was performed by "mammets" (another term in use for the wooden representatives of heroes), as well as the *Duke of Guise,* a name that was perhaps given to Marlow's *Massacre of Paris,*† or it may refer to a tra-

* The manner in which puppet-shows were represented in Spain, is very clearly described in chap. xxvi. of the second part of *Don Quixote.* Peter there worked the figures, and his boy interpreted, though not to the knight's satisfaction. The fable in that instance was purely romantic, but sacred subjects were at least as common.

† Henslowe probably refers to this play, as "the tragedy of the Guyes," in his papers. See Mal. Sh. by Boswell, iii. 299.

gedy by Webster under that title.* If inference were·
not sufficient, testimony might be adduced, to shew
that the puppets were clothed as nearly as possible
like the actors at the regular theatres in those plays
which were thought fit subjects for the "motions."
The minute fidelity of Ben Jonson to the manners of
his day, in depicting the "humours" of his characters,
has led him in several places to introduce the name
of a principal proprietor of puppet-shows, who was
known by the title of Captain Pod. He mentions
him in his *Every Man out of his Humour*,† as well as in
his Epigrams,‡ from which last it also appears that the
word "motion," which properly means the representation by puppets, was sometimes applied to the
figures employed in the performance.§

---

* See the Dedication to Webster's *White Devil*, as quoted
in note ‡ in the new edition of *Dodsley's Old Plays*, vol. vi. 207.

† "Nay, rather let him be Captain Pod, and this his motion,
for he does nothing but shew him." (Act iv. Scene 4.)

‡ The title of the Epigram is "On the new motion" —

"See you yond motion? not the old fa-ding,
    Nor Captain Pod, nor yet the Eltham thing," &c.

§ Thus also "Speed," in the *Two Gentlemen of Verona*, exclaims, "O excellent *motion!* O exceeding *puppet!* now will
he *interpret* to her." (Act ii. Scene 1.)

The formidable rivalship of puppet-plays to the regular drama at a later date is established by the fact,
that the proprietors of the theatres in Drury Lane, and
near Lincoln's Inn Fields, formerly petitioned Charles
II. that a puppet-show stationed on the present site
of Cecil Street in the Strand, might not be allowed to
exhibit, or might be removed to a greater distance, as
its attractiveness materially interfered with the pros-
perity of their concerns. It is not unlikely that burlesque and ridicule were sometimes aimed at the productions of the regular stage by the exhibitors of
" motions."

There is little doubt that the most ancient puppet-
shows, like the Mysteries, dealt in stories taken from
the Old and New Testament, or from the lives and
legends of Saints. Towards the end of the reign
of Elizabeth, as we have seen, historical and other
fables began to be treated by them ; but still scriptural
subjects were commonly exhibited, and Shakspeare,
in the quotation we have made from his *Winter's Tale*,
mentions that of the " Prodigal Son." Perhaps, none
was more popular than " Nineveh, with Jonas and the
Whale : " it is noticed by Ben Jonson twice in the
same play *(Every Man out of his Humour)*, and not
less than twenty other authors speak of it. From a
passage in Cowley's *Cutter of Coleman Street* (Act v.

Sc. ii.), we collect that even the puritans, with all their zealous hatred of the "profane stages," did not object to be present at its "holy performance." The motion of "Babylon" is also frequently noticed; but "London" and "Rome" likewise figured in the metropolis at the same time. Fleet Street and Holborn Bridge, both great thoroughfares, were the usual places where puppet-plays were exhibited in the reign of Elizabeth;* and the authority of Butler has been quoted by Mr. Gifford (Ben Jonson, ii. 46, note) to shew that Fleet Street continued to be infested by "motions" and "monsters" at least down to the Restoration. Scriptural motions were not wholly laid aside within the last fifty or sixty years; and Goldsmith, in his comedy, *She Stoops to Conquer*, refers to the display of Solomon's Temple in a puppet-show. The current joke (at what date it originated seems uncertain) of Punch popping his head from behind the side curtain, and addressing the Patriarch in his ark, while the floods were pouring down, with "hazy weather, master Noah," †

* *Motions* were also frequently exhibited at Brentford : Mayne, and other old dramatists, speak of city wives going thither to see them.

† This might very well belong to Piron's *Arlequin Deucalion*, mentioned in a note in the preceding chapter. Perhaps, the joke was derived from thence.

proves that, at one period, the adventures of the hero of comparatively modern exhibitions of the kind were combined with stories selected from the Bible.

The late Mr. Joseph S. Strutt, in his "Sports and Pastimes of the People of England," thus speaks of the puppet-shows in his time. "In my memory these shows consisted of a wretched display of wooden figures, barbarously formed and decorated, without the least degree of taste or propriety: the wires that communicated the motion to them appeared at the top of their heads, and the manner in which they were made to move evinced the ignorance and inattention of the managers. The dialogues were mere jumbles of absurdities and nonsense, intermixed with low immoral discourses, passing between Punch and the fiddler, for the orchestra rarely admitted of more than one minstrel; and these flashes of merriment were made offensive to decency by the actions of the puppet."*

From whatever cause the change may have arisen, certain it is, that, at present, in the ordinary exhibitions of "Punch and Judy," the breaches of decorum complained of by Mr. Strutt are rare and slight. He

* Page 152, edit. 1810. We are glad to see that a new edition of this learned and entertaining work is about to be printed in a convenient 8vo. form, under the care of Mr. Hone.

afterwards proceeds as follows: "In the present day, the puppet-showman travels about the streets, when the weather will permit, and carries the motions, with the theatre itself, upon his back. The exhibition takes place in the open air, and the precarious income of the miserable itinerant depends entirely on the voluntary contribution of the spectators, which, as far as one may judge from the squalid appearance he usually makes, is very trifling."

We have never seen less than two men concerned in these ambulatory exhibitions: one to carry the theatre and use Punch's tin whistle, and the other to bear the box of puppets and blow the trumpet. During the performance the money is collected from the bystanders: the "squalid appearance" of the proprietors is part of their business, and, far from agreeing with Mr. Strutt that the contributions are "very trifling," we have seen, for we have taken the pains to ascertain it, two or three and four shillings obtained at each repetition; so that supposing only ten performances take place in a summer's day, the reward to the two men on an average might be about fifteen shillings each. On one occasion, we remember to have seen three different spectators give sixpence, besides the halfpence elsewhere contributed ; on which the collector went back to the theatre and whis-

pered the exhibitor, who immediately made Punch
thus address the crowd: "Ladies and Gentlemen, I
never yet played for sevenpence halfpenny, and I
never will; so good morning." He then "struck his
tent" and departed; pocketing nearly two shillings,
and excusing himself from going through the performance, under pretence that all the contributions
he had received only amounted to sevenpence halfpenny.

CHAPTER III.

ARRIVAL OF PUNCH IN ENGLAND.

WE now come to a point of great national importance —when Punch made his *début*, or first appearance, in England. Great events are usually recorded on the page of history, but this is one, that, by some strange fatality, has escaped all notice; and, after the lapse of more than a century, we have been called upon to examine forgotten records, and to furnish detailed information. The documents in the State Paper Office, the Records in the Tower, the Rolls of Parliament, and the MSS. in the British Museum, and in the Libraries of the Universities, we are sorry to observe, have supplied us with no intelligence regarding Mr. Punch, Mrs. Judy, or any other member of his family. We have also patiently gone through Evelyn's and Pepys's Diaries, with many other works of the same kind, in print and out of print; but though they dwell on the fire of London, the plague, declarations of war, treaties of peace, the reception of ambassadors, and other historical trifles of that sort, they are silent regarding the arrival of this illustrious foreigner.

Dr. Drake (and a great many writers before him, for he seldom runs the risk of advancing a novelty) has called the reign of Queen Anne "the Augustan Age of Literature" in England.* Its claim to this proud distinction has been disputed, and certain admirers of old prose and poetry have set up the reign of Elizabeth in opposition to it. Now, although *non nostrum tantas componere lites*, if we can clearly establish, that the puppet-show of "Punch and Judy" was well known and much admired, while

"Our gracious Anne was Queen of Britain's Isle;"

if he reached this country a little before that period, and if the refined theatrical entertainment he offered, so well suited to a highly polished and enlightened nation, were then popular, it will, we think, turn the scale at once, and settle the question for ever. †

---

* See his "Essays illustrative of the Tatler, Spectator, and Guardian," i. p. 32.

† We have already seen that Nash mentions Harlequin before the year 1600; but we afterwards lose sight of him, by

We find frequent mention of him in the Tatler; and even the "classical Addison" does not scruple, in the Spectator, to introduce a regular criticism upon one

that name, for three quarters of a century. Dryden notices him; and Ravenscroft, in 1677, reproduced him upon the stage, in a piece called "Scaramouch a Philosopher, Harlequin a School-boy, Bravo, Merchant and Magician."—He calls it "a comedy after the Italian manner;" and in the prologue he professes to have used Molière's *Fourberies de Scapin*, which he might not have acknowledged, had not Otway been just beforehand with him. However, Ravenscroft had the good sense to adopt the two best scenes of the French play, which Otway omitted, and which Molière himself borrowed from *de Bergerac*. Ravenscroft's play includes not only the Harlequin, but the Doctor, the Scaramouch, and the Captain of the Italian *impromptu* comedy. The latter is called *Spitzaferro*, and is described as "a coward, ignorant and bold," of the same species as the Captain Matamoros (or *Moor-killer*), in which Silvio Fiorillo, the inventor of Pulcinella, was so famous as always to pass by that title. The Spanish Captain was brought upon the stage while the Spaniards had possession of Naples in the end of the 15th and beginning of the 16th centuries; but, as he was intended to ridicule that nation, of course he originated in some other part of Italy. After 1677, we have no distinct notice of Harlequin in England, until 1719, when a mock-opera called "Harlequin Hydaspes" was acted at Lincoln's Inn Fields' Theatre. Cibber, in his "Apology," gives a full account of the use Rich subsequently made of him, in opposition to the regular drama.

of the performances of Punch. As the Tatler was published earlier in point of date,* we will begin by referring to the notices of the same notorious and amusing actor by Sir Richard Steele. Dr. Johnson was one of the first, if not the very first, to broach the notion that his age had become too wise for the periodicals of Queen Anne's time;† as if, supposing the fact to be so, there was nothing else to be gained from the lucubrations of the wittiest and ablest men of that day, but their out-of-date learning. The effect has been, with the co-operation of no small share of self-conceit in the present generation, to throw the best of our essayists far into the shade; and the Tatler, Spectator, and Guardian, are now considered works very well for the period at which they were written, but far behind the rapid "march of intellect" during the last forty or fifty years. On this account we shall not content ourselves with bare references, because we are aware, that many of those who read our pages will not have the contemned productions we have named within their reach.

The great exhibitor of Punch immortalized, we will

---

* The first number is dated April 12, 1709: the first number of the Spectator is dated March 1, 1710–11.
† See Dr. Johnson's Life of Addison.

say, by Steele, notwithstanding the disesteem into
which that delightful writer has fallen, is Mr. Powell;
and in No. 44 of the Tatler, Isaac Bickerstaff, Esq.,
complains that he had been abused by Punch in a
Prologue, supposed to be spoken by him, but really
delivered by his master, who stood behind, "worked
the wires," and, by "a thread in one of Punch's chops,"
gave to him the appearance of enunciation. These expressions are important, inasmuch as they shew a
method of performance and a degree of intricacy in the
machinery not now known. At present the puppets
are played only by putting the hand under the dress,
and making the middle finger and thumb serve for
the arms, while the forefinger works the head. The
opening and shutting of the mouth is a refinement
which does not seem to be practised in Italy; and it
will be seen by a quotation we shall make presently from another contemporary work, that Powell's
puppets were "jointed." No. 50 of the Tatler contains a real or supposed letter from the showman
himself at Bath, insisting upon his right of control
over his own puppets, and denying all knowledge of
"the original of puppet-shows; and the several
changes and revolutions that have happened in them
since Thespis." A subsequent number (115) is curious, as it shews that such was the rivalship of

Punch in point of attractiveness, particularly with the ladies, that the Opera and the celebrated singer Nicolini were almost deserted in his favour. Nicolini and the Opera were ridiculed, as we find from other sources, by the squeakings of a pig, well instructed for the purpose, and who had been also taught to dance. From the Tatler we learn, that then, as now, Punchinello (for he is so designated and dignified) had " a scolding wife," and that he was attended, besides, by a number of courtiers and nobles.

Powell's show was set up in Covent Garden, opposite to St. Paul's Church; and the Spectator (No. 14*) contains the letter of the sexton, who complained that the performances of Punch thinned the congregation in the church, and that, as Powell exhibited during the time of prayers, the tolling of the bell was taken, by all who heard it, for notice of the intended commencement of the exhibition. The writer of the paper then proceeds, in another epistle, to establish that the puppet-show was much superior to the opera of *Rinaldo and Armida,* represented at the Haymarket, and to observe, that " too much encouragement could not be given to Mr. Powell's skill in *motions.*" A regular

* Attributed to Steele, who had the good taste to be delighted with Mr. Punch.

parallel is drawn between the two, which ends most decidedly in favour of Powell in every respect but the inferior point of the moral.*

But the most curious and particular information regarding Powell and his performances, is contained in a small work published in London in 1715, professing to give an account of his life: it is entitled "A Second Tale of a Tub; or the History of Robert Powell, the Puppet-show-man;" but it is, in fact, a political satire on Sir Robert Walpole, to whose life and administration nearly all the adventures are made applicable. It is preceded by a copper-plate, in which that celebrated minister, in a court dress, is represented as the master and interpreter of a puppet-show: he stands below, with a stick to point to the different characters; behind is the stage, lighted with foot-lamps, on which stand a male and a female puppet, the male having a very lofty conical cap, a large ruff, and a considerable paunch (but without the long nose which

* Penkethman, an actor, and the head of a strolling company, often praised for his low humour in the reign of Anne, seems also at one time to have been master of a puppet-show of some kind; but as so remarkable a personage as Punch is not mentioned, it is supposed that it was confined to an exhibition of the "heathen gods," as noticed in No. 31 of the Spectator.

distinguishes Punch); and the female in a very plain
dress with a falling band. The Dedication particularly
refers to the extreme popularity of Powell, to his exhibitions at Bath, and in Covent Garden, and then
proceeds thus:

"It would be trifling, after this, to recount to you
how Mr. Powell has melted a whole audience into
pity and tears, when he has made the poor starved
Children in the Wood miserably depart in peace, and a
Robin bury them. It would be tedious to enumerate
how often he has made Punch the diversion of all the
spectators, by putting into his mouth many bulls and
flat contradictions, to the dear joy of all true Teagues.
Or to what end should I attempt to describe how
heroically he makes *King Bladud* perform the part of
a British Prince."

In the body of the work, after going through the
supposed adventures of Powell, he reduces him at
last to a puppet-showman, and thus continues:

"Now was he (Powell) resolved to get actors that
should speak and move as he pleased. The first he hired
was one *Punch*, a comical, staring, gaping, noisy fellow.
Punch was soon attended by a whole train of diminutive actors, of both sexes, viz., jointed kings, queens,
waiting-maids, virgins, babies, noblemen, baboons,
tumblers, aldermen, rope-dancers, geese, country-

squires, rats, lord mayors, footmen, sows, Indians, cats, conjurers, owls, priests, brazen heads, robin-red-breasts, and elders, all of which were assisted by a wise interpreter; so Mr. Powell had quickly a full stage. In short, he was mightily frequented by all sorts of quality, and Punch, with his gang, soon broke the strollers, and enjoyed the city of Bath by themselves. Money coming in a-pace, Mr. Powell bought him several new scenes, for the diversion of his audience and the better acting of several incomparable dramas of his own composing, such as *Whittington and his Cat, the Children in the Wood, Dr. Faustus, Friar Bacon and Friar Bungay, Robin Hood and Little John, Mother Shipton, Mother Goose,* together with the pleasant and comical humours of Valentini, Nicolini, and the tuneful warbling pig, of Italian race."

Nearly all the humour of the application to Sir Robert Walpole, of the "Second Tale of a Tub," is now lost; but the anonymous author seems to have possessed some wit, and was much better acquainted with the ancient as well as modern drama of this country, than most of his contemporaries.

From these sources we collect, most distinctly, that the popularity of Punch was completely established, and that he triumphed over all his rivals, materially

lessening the receipts at least at the Opera, if not at the
regular national theatres; and accomplishing, at that
period, by his greater attractiveness, what Dennis, by
his "Essay on Operas after the Italian manner," and
other *critiques de profession,* had been unable to effect.
He could hardly have taken such firm possession of
the public mind if he had only recently emigrated
from his native country; and no writer of the reign
of Queen Anne, who notices him at all, speaks of him
as a novelty. This may be established from poetry
as well as prose. Gay, in his "Shepherd's Week —
Saturday," distinguishes between the tricks of "Jack
Pudding in his parti-coloured jacket," and "Punch's
feats," and tells us that they were both well known
at rustic wakes and fairs: but perhaps the most remarkable account of our hero is to be found among
Swift's humorous political pieces, in "A Dialogue between mad Mullinix and Timothy;" regarding which
personages, it is not necessary for us to insert explana-
tions, which may easily be found elsewhere. A description of a puppet-show, as it then was exhibited, is
introduced by way of illustration; and from our extract,
(with one omission, only, for the sake of decorum,) it
will be seen that it possessed the recommendation of
extraordinary variety.

" Observe, the audience is in pain
While Punch is hid behind the scene,
But when they hear his rusty voice,
With what impatience they rejoice !
And then they value not two straws
How Solomon decides the cause ;
Which the true mother, — which pretender,
Nor listen to the witch of Endor.
Should Faustus, with the Devil behind him,
Enter the stage, they never mind him ;
If Punch, to stir their fancy, shews
In at the door his monstrous nose,
Then sudden draws it back again,
Oh! what a pleasure mix'd with pain!
You every moment think an age,
Till he appears upon the stage :
And first himself you see him clap
Upon the Queen of Sheba's lap.
The Duke of Lorraine drew his sword :
Punch roaring ran, and running roar'd,
Reviles all people in his jargon,
And sells the King of Spain a bargain :
St. George himself he plays the wag on,
And mounts astride upon the dragon :
He gets a thousand thumps and kicks,
Yet cannot leave his roguish tricks ;
In every action thrusts his nose, —
The reason why no mortal knows.
There's not a puppet made of wood
But what would hang him, if they could ;

> While, teazing all, by all he's teaz'd,
> How well are the spectators pleas'd;
> Who in the *motion* have no share,
> But purely come to hear and stare;
> Have no concern for Sabra's sake
> Which gets the better, saint or snake,
> Provided Punch, for there's the jest,
> Be soundly maul'd and plague the rest." *

How Punch, King Solomon, Dr. Faustus,† the Queen of Sheba, the Duke of Lorraine, St. George, and the rest of the characters, were brought together, we have no precise knowledge; but "time and space" were evidently "annihilated, to make *spectators* happy." No wonder that such exhibitions thinned the theatres, and kept the churches empty.

Although our information may be considered complete, as to the high favour in which Punch was then held by the multitude, we are still, and shall probably

---

* If the curious reader wishes for it, he will find a history of this poem in the eighth number of the "Intelligencer."

† Many authorities might be adduced to shew that Dr. Faustus often formed a member of the puppet company. See Pope's "Dunciad," III. 1. 307; C. Pitt's "Prologue to the Strollers;" A. Hill's "Answer to an Epistle from Mrs. Robinson," &c. According to the author of the "Second Tale of a Tub," one of Powell's shows was called *Doctor Faustus;* and Mountford, the actor, produced a farce under the same title in 1697.

remain, without any positive intelligence regarding the exact date when he arrived in England. We think, nevertheless, that we may conclude from all the premises with tolerable safety, that he and King William came in together, and that the Revolution is to be looked upon as the era of the introduction of the illustrious Family of Punch, and of the "glorious House of Orange."* Certain it is that the Dutch were extremely celebrated for their skill in mechanics; and the author of the "Second Tale of a Tub," 1715, bears witness, in the Dedication, that "the Dutch were the most expert nation in the world for puppet-shows."

That the dress and appearance of Punch, in 1731, were as nearly as possible like what they now are, will be seen by the following popular song, extracted from vol. vi. of "The Musical Miscellany," printed in that

---

* There is, however, a passage in Grainger's Biog. Hist. iv. 350, which, if taken literally, as perhaps it is not meant to be, would shew that Punch was known in England before the abdication of James II. He is speaking of a notorious Merry-Andrew, of the name of Phillips, who, he says, "was some time fiddler to a puppet-show, in which capacity he held many a dialogue with *Punch*, in much the same strain as he did afterwards with the mountebank Doctor, his master, on the stage. This Zany being regularly educated, had confessedly the advantage of his brethren."

year.* In other respects it is a curious production, and, perhaps, was sung by Punch himself, in one of his entertainments. It is inserted under the title of,

PUNCHINELLO.

Trade's awry, so am I,
　　As well as some folks that are greater;
But by the peace we at present enjoy
　　We hope to be richer and straighter.
Bribery must be laid aside,
　　To somebody's mortification:
He that is guilty, Oh, let him be tried,
　　And expos'd for a rogue to the nation.
　　　　I'm that little fellow
　　　　Call'd Punchinello,
Much beauty I carry about me;
　　　I'm witty and pretty,
　　　And come to delight ye;
You cannot be merry without me.

---

* In 1735, was published the third edition of *Harlequin Horace, or the Art of Modern Poetry*, dedicated to the celebrated John Rich; one object of which is to shew that Pantomime had driven poetry from the stage. A frontispiece represents Harlequin and Punch uniting their efforts to expel Apollo, who, with his lyre, is making his *exit* from the theatre, Punch giving the god a parting kick. The dress of Punch is very nearly the same as at present, with the exception of the conical hat, which has a sort of brim to it.

My cap is like a sugar-loaf,
And round my collar I wear a ruff;
I'd strip and shew you my shape in buff,
     But fear the ladies would flout me.
My rising back and distorted breast,
Whene'er I shew 'em, become a jest;
And, all in all, I am one of the best,
     So nobody need doubt me.

Æsop was a monstrous slave,
  And waited at Xanthus's table;
Yet he was always a comical knave,
  And an excellent dab at a fable.
So when I presume to shew
  My shape, I am just such another;
By my sweet looks and good humour, I know,
  You must take me for him or his brother.
     The fair and the comely
     May think me but homely,
  Because I am tawney and crooked;
     But he that by nature
     Is taller and straighter,
  May happen to prove a blockhead.

But I, fair ladies, am full as wise,
As he that tickles your ears with lies,
And thinks he pleases your charming eyes
     With a rat-tail wig and a cockade:
I mean the bully that never fought,
Yet dresses himself in a scarlet coat,
Without a commission — not worth a groat, —
     But struts with an empty pocket.

It deserves remark, that Punch has not always been a mere puppet in the British empire; for in the Biographia Dramatica there is an entry of a farce called *Punch turned Schoolmaster*, which we have not been able to obtain, and therefore cannot speak of the nature or conduct of it. The date of its representation is not ascertained, but a prologue for it was written by Sheridan, and printed in 1724. The performances of M. Mazurier in 1825, in the "Shipwreck of Pulcinella, or the Neapolitan Nuptials," are so well remembered, that it is needless to do more than allude to them.

CHAPTER IV.

NATURE OF PUNCH'S PERFORMANCES.

WHAT was the dialogue of any of the pieces in which Pulcinella originally performed, soon after his invention, cannot now be distinctly ascertained. We have already seen that they were called *commedie à soggetto* and *commedie all'improviso*, or *impromptu* and *extempore* comedies, the plot and arrangement of which were first communicated to the actors, who afterwards filled up the dialogue according to their own notions, as their wit or invention might serve them.* The

---

* The Reader who wishes for further knowledge upon this subject, may either consult D'Israeli's Cur. Lit. iii. 25, or the authorities from which he derived his statements, Gimma's *Italia Letterata*, Signorelli's *Storia Critica de' Teatri*, &c., and Riccoboni.

schemes, or, as the Italians call them, *canevas* and *scenarie,* of some pieces of this description were printed early in the 16th century, by Flamineo Scala, and others, appeared in 1661, but not a syllable of what passed between any of the characters is there supplied. Hence almost every thing must depend upon conjecture; but the probability certainly is, that actors of this class, accustomed repeatedly to perform together, would, ere long, come to a perfect understanding with each other, and the interlocutions thus acquire a certain degree of permanence, until some change took place in the company.* At different places the same plot would be represented, and, of course, the same dialogue would be sufficient, as far as it could be remembered. No doubt, the dramas consisted of "gross buffooneries," because the actors were *buffone;* but

---

* Ruzzante was a very famous comedian in the opening of the 16th century, and printed various comedies and dialogues, which he set down from his own invention and from the mouths of the extempore performers (of whom he was one) as the language became habitual: he is mentioned as the first who put different Italian dialects into the mouths of his performers. *Il Travaglia* by Andrea Calmo, printed at Venice in 1557, also professes to be *di varie lingue adornata.* Riccoboni informs us that Scaramouche, Harlequin, and other characters, threw off their provincialism on occasion, and *tous declament des vers en bon Romain.*

there was room for the display of ready talent; and if a
few of the pieces had been left upon record, we should
most likely have found that they had something else
to recommend them besides the coarseness of their
jokes, delivered in the dialect of Italy peculiar to each
of the characters.*

* The actors, whether representing the Neapolitan *Pulcinella*, the Calabrian *Giangurgolo*, or the Milanese *Beltrame*, preserved the dialect of their respective countries. The Spanish
Captain spoke a language compounded of Italian and Spanish.
Of the dialect employed by Punch, and by the country people
of Acerra (of whom he was originally supposed to be one), we
have a specimen in a three act comedy, called *Pulcinella finto
Dottore*, which was acted at Rome during the Carnival of 1728.
A very short extract will suffice, as the language is sometimes
scarcely intelligible to a native. *Flamineo*, a young lover, is
endeavouring to persuade his servant, *Pulcinella*, to assume the
dress and appearance of Doctor *Farfallone*, his rival, in order
to impose upon the father of the lady.

Flam. E possibile, che non ti dia l'animo di dire queste
quattro parole?

Pul. Ne diraggio cinquanta, bene mio, mà se tu struppei do
discurso.

Flam. E come dirai?

Pul. Diraggio cà songo venuto dalla Cierra per nzorarme.

Flam. E ti chiami?

Pul. Purcenella.

Flam. O stordito! ed ecco atterrata tutta la machina.

Neither in England have we the means of knowing, with precision, the nature of the earlier exhibitions of "Punch and his merry family." How the stories of Mr. Powell were compounded, as far as relates to the dialogue, must remain a mystery, the writers of his day never entering into this interesting point. It appears from the Spectator (No. 14), that under the little Piazza, in Covent Garden, Mr. Powell's hero danced a minuet with "a well-disciplined pig"; which, according to the "Second Tale of a Tub," had been taught also to ridicule the celebrated Italian singers, Valentini and Nicolini; and in the same show, "King Harry (probably the Eighth) laid his leg upon the Queen's lap in too ludicrous a manner." We likewise learn on this authority, as well as from Swift, that, at that time, Punch possessed the same animating voice which, when heard in our streets, still lights up the eyes of the rising generation.

The Spectator, and the "Second Tale of a Tub," may further be brought forward, to prove that

Pul. E peche?

Flam. E perche tu hai du dire che sei il Dottore, venuto da Bologna, e ti chiami Farfallone.

Pul. E ca non buoglio rinega lo pajeso mio, e poi chillo nome de Farfantone non c'aggio genio nente, cà fete no tantillo di galera, &c.

"Whittington and his Cat"* was one of the subjects chosen by Mr. Powell for the display of his talents. We take it for granted, that in all these cases, as at the present moment, the dialogue was extemporaneous, excepting in so far as it became habitual and mechanical by frequent repetition. That singing then formed part of the entertainment, is not mere matter of inference, and we know that it did so in the time of Strutt, who also speaks of a fiddler, now discontinued: many living can remember the introduction of "snatches of old songs," and parodies of popular ballards by Punch. Steele makes mention of Powell's "books"; but, in all likelihood, they were not books of his performances, which in our day, and for our purpose, would be great curiosities.

* It has, we believe, been hitherto thought that the story of "Whittington, thrice Lord Mayor of London," was exclusively national; but supposing the notion to be well founded, what we are about to mention affords one more proof to those already furnished of late years, that, in time, tales of the kind become the common property of other countries. It is found among the *Facezie, Motti, Buffonerie, et Burle* of the Piovano Arlotto, which were originally printed very early in the 16th century, and subsequently were re-issued from the celebrated press of the Giunti, at Florence, in 1565. The title it there bears is this: *Il Piovano, à un prete che fece mercantia di palle, dice la novella delle gatte.* With a change of persons and places, it is the same story as our own "Whittington and his Cat."

At all events, there is certain ground for concluding that the adventures of Punch, as represented in this country, did not by any means always consist of that series in which they are now usually performed; and although we are not in a condition to adduce distinct proof upon the point, we cannot help thinking that the introduction and popularity of "Don Juan" contributed mainly to the arrangement of the performance as it is now daily exhibited.* We have consulted some persons, whose age is sufficiently advanced to enable them to supply the information, and they agree, that about that period the character of Punch certainly underwent a material change. Although we are inclined to favour this hypothesis, we must allow that the story, as displayed on some parts of the continent at the present moment, bears many features of strong resemblance to the fable of the piece as shewn in Great Britain.† We here advert to Punch in the puppet-show, and not on the stage in Italy.

* Hone, in his account of the "Mysteries," &c. draws a parallel between the two; but, in order to render it more obvious, he a little perverts the story of Punch, particularly in the catastrophe.

† It seems hardly likely that this change was earliest effected in Italy; for when Goldoni brought out his *Don Juan*, he for the first time left out Harlequin, and introduced other comic characters in his place, as he himself informs us in his Memoirs

The original of "Don Juan" is generally allowed to be Spanish : in that language, it is called *Il Convidado di Pietra,* and its author was Tirso de Molina. It was played in Paris first by the Italian company ; and to rival them an actor of the name of Villiers brought it out in French verse, at another theatre, while the biographers of Molière inform us that he wrote his *Festin de Pierre* in prose, because he was in such haste to anticipate Villiers. T. Corneille added rhymes to it on the death of Molière. Three years afterwards, viz., in 1676, it first appeared on the English stage, from the pen of Shadwell ; but Punch was, probably, then unknown here, at least by that appellation, and the change in the fable, to which we have referred, was occasioned, if at all, long afterwards, by the extreme popularity of the pantomime-ballets at the Royalty, and subsequently at Drury Lane Theatre, about forty years ago.*

(vol. i. p. 311, edit. Paris 1787). In the *Convidado di Pietra,* to which the Italians had been accustomed, Harlequin on one occasion saves himself by swimming, with the aid of a couple of bladders. Sacchi was the most famous Harlequin of his day, and is highly extolled by Goldoni, who wrote several pieces expressly for him.

* "Don Juan" was acted at the Royalty Theatre in 1787, and at Drury Lane in 1790. They were played many nights in succession, and are hardly yet laid aside.

The ensuing ballad was written very nearly about that date, being extracted from a curious collection of comic and serious pieces of the kind, in print and manuscript, with the figures 1791, 1792, and 1793, in various parts of it, as the times, probably, when the individual who made it obtained the copies he transcribed, or inserted in their original shape. It certainly affords evidence of the connection between the stories of Punch and Don Juan; and (like the old ballads of "King Lear and his Three Daughters," "The Spanish Tragedy, or the lamentable murder of Horatio and Bellimperia," &c.) was perhaps founded upon the performance, by one who had witnessed and was highly gratified by it. It is called,

PUNCH'S PRANKS.

Oh! harken now to me awhile,
  A story I will tell you
Of Mr. Punch, who was a vile
  Deceitful murderous fellow:
Who had a wife, a child also, —
  And both of matchless beauty;
The infant's name I do not know,
  Its mother's name was Judy.
           Right tol de rol lol, &c.

But not so handsome Mr. Punch,
  Who had a monstrous nose, Sir;
And on his back there grew a hunch,
  That to his head arose, Sir:
But then, they say, that he could speak
  As winning as a Mermaid,
And by his voice—a treble squeak, —
  He Judy won, that fair maid.

But he was cruel as a Turk,
  Like Turk, was discontented,
To have one wife—'twas poorish work—
  But still the law prevented
His having two, or twenty-two,
  Tho' he for all was ready;
So what did he in that case do?
  Oh! sad!—he kept a lady.

Now Mrs. Judy found it out,
  And being very jealous,
She pull'd her husband by the snout,
  His lady gay as well as.
Then Punch he in a passion flew,
  And took it so in dudgeon,
He fairly split her head in two,
  Oh! monster!—with a bludgeon.

And next he took his little heir,
  Oh, most unnat'ral father!
And flung it out of a two pair
  Window; for he'd rather

Possess the lady of his love,
    Than lady of the law, Sir,
And car'd not for his child above
    A pinch of Maccabau, Sir.

His wife's relations came to town
    To ask of him the cause, Sir :
He took his stick and knock'd 'em down,
    And serv'd 'em the same sauce, Sir :
And said, the law was not *his* law,
    He car'd not for a letter;
And if on him it laid its claw,
    He'd teach it to know better.

Then took to travel o'er each land,
    So loving and seductive,
Three ladies only could withstand
    His lessons most instructive.
The first, a simple rustic maid ;
    The next, a pious abbess ;
The third I'd call, but I'm afraid,
    The tabbiest of tabbies.*

----

*In this stanza, the writer (we regret that so pleasant an
effusion should be anonymous) seems to have had in his mind
Spenser's Squire of Dames (*Fairy Queen,* B. iii. canto 7),
who had been commanded by his mistress to go forth "a colo-
nelling," against the virtue of the female sex. He returned
in less than a year, with tokens of three hundred conquests ;
and she then set him a penance to bring testimonies of as

In Italy, the dames were worst;
 In France, they were too clamorous;
In England, altho' coy at first,
 Yet after quite as amorous.
In Spain, they all were proud, yet frail;
 In Germany, but coolish;
But further north he did not sail,
 To do so had been foolish.

In all his course he scrupled not
 To make a jest of murder,
So fathers, brothers, went to pot:—
 It really makes one shudder
To think upon the horrid track
 Of blood he shed on system;
And, though with hump upon his back,
 The dames could not resist him.

----

many women who had resisted his arts and entreaties. In
three years, he had only found three.

 " The first which then refused me," said he,
  " Certes was but a common courtesane,
 Yet, flat refus'd to have a-do with me,
  Because I could not give her many a Jane."
(Thereat full heartily laugh'd Satyrane.)
  " The second was an holy nun to chose,
 Which would not let me be her chapelaine,
  Because she knew, she said, I would disclose
Her counsel if she should her trust in me repose.

  " The third a damsel was of low degree,
 Whom I in country cottage found by chance," &c.

'Tis said, that he a compact sign'd
   With one they call "Old Nich'las";
But if I knew them, I've no mind
   To go into partic'lars.
To it, perhaps, he ow'd success
   Wherever he might go, Sir;
But I believe we must confess,
   The ladies were so so, Sir.

At last he back to England came,
   A jolly rake and rover,
And pass'd him by another name,
   An *alias*, when at Dover.
But soon the police laid a scheme,
   To clap him into prison:
They took him, when he least could dream
   Of such a fate as his'n.*

And now the day was drawing near,
   The day of retribution;
The trial o'er, he felt but queer
   At thought of execution.
But when the hangman, all so grim,
   Declar'd that all was ready,
Punch only tipp'd the wink at him,
   And ask'd after his lady.

---

* This sounds like an ignorant vulgarism; but it is, in fact, only an abbreviation, *per ellipsin*, of *his own*. We find it applied to the pronoun *her* in G. Chapman's *Humorous Day's Mirth*, a comedy printed in 1599, sign: G.

   "What shall I do at sight of her and *her'n?*"

Pretending he knew not the use
 Of rope he saw from tree, Sir,
The hangman's head into the noose
 He got, while he got free, Sir.
At last, the Devil came to claim
 His own; but Punch what *he* meant
Demanded, and denied the same;
 He knew no such agreement!

"You don't! (the Devil cried:) 'tis well;
 I'll quickly let you know it:"
And so to furious work they fell,
 As hard as they could go it.
The Devil with his pitch-fork fought,
 While Punch had but a stick, Sir,
But kill'd the Devil,* as he ought.
 Huzza! there's no Old Nick, Sir.
     Right tol de rol lol, &c.

In a previous part of this chapter, we have established, that Dr. Faustus was a principal character in

* "To kill the Devil," and "to drive the Devil into his own dominions," *cacciar il Diavolo nell' inferno,* meant the same thing in Italian, as is fully explained in Boccacio, as well as Sacchetti (Nov. 101), and in Bandello (Nov. 9, vol. i. edit. Ven. 1566). It is only used in English in its literal sense, and it is, of course, so to be understood in this ballad. In its figurative application, perhaps no hero, not even Don Juan himself, oftener was the death of his Satanic Majesty than Punch. More we cannot say.

puppet-shows of that date;* and every body knows
from the old Romance† and from Goethe's Drama,
if not from Marlow's tragedy, that that renowned
conjuror had entered into a similar bond with the
potentate of the infernal regions. There may be,
therefore, some link of connection between Powell's
performance and that upon which the preceding ballad
has been framed, which in the lapse of a century
has been lost. In our day, we hear nothing of such
a compact; but the Devil is brought in to carry
away the hero to the punishment merited by his
boasted crimes. In this respect, we should rather

---

* Mountford, the stage Adonis of his day, in 1697, wrote
what was at that time called "a Farce," on the Life and Death
of Dr. Faustus, in which Harlequin and Scaramouch both
figured, but nothing is said of Punch in it. Lee and Jevon,
two distinguished comic performers, took the parts of Harlequin and Scaramouch, and it seems to have met with success,
as, after having been acted in Dorset Gardens, it was revived
at the Theatre in Lincoln's Inn Fields.

† An elegant reprint of it, under the care of Mr. Thoms, has
recently made a scarce and curious work very accessible. We
will take this opportunity of pointing out an error in the Introduction (p. viii.) where Marlow's Tragedy is spoken of as if
it had first appeared in 1610. Marlow was killed in 1593 (before the date assigned by Mr. Thoms to "the Second Report
of Dr. Faustus"), and his play was printed in 1604. We know
of no edition in 1610.

have taken Punch for a Frenchman than an Italian, according to the opinion of old Heylin; who, speaking of our near neighbours, and of that vanity which, when he wrote, made them vaunt of their vices, exclaims, in a sort of uncharitable rapture, "foolish and most perishing wretches, by whom each several wickedness is twice committed: first in the act, and secondly in the boast!"*

* "France painted to the Life" — London, 1656, p. 53, with the motto *Quid non Gallia parturit ingens*. Dante was no great admirer of the French, whom he thinks only just better than the people of Sienna:

> ———— *Hor fugiammai*
> *Gente si vand coma la Sanese?*
> *Certo non la Francesca si d'assai.*
>
> *Inf.* c. xxix.

CHAPTER V.

THE MORAL OF PUNCH'S PERFORMANCES, &c.

POETICAL justice is a matter upon which the most sagacious critics have insisted; and it cannot be denied that, in the ordinary exhibitions, which go by the name of "Punch and Judy," it is decidedly violated. One great object, as they contend, of dramatic poetry ought to be to enforce a moral; and, if we try the species of scenic representation now under our view by that test, we shall find it unquestionably deficient. It is nevertheless a point capable of dispute, whether people were ever made better or worse by theatrical performances: for instance, whether a single apprentice was ever deterred or reclaimed from vice by all the sombre repetitions of George Barnwell, at Easter and Christmas. The old lawyer, who used to send his clerks to witness every execution, with the admonition,

"There, you rogues, go to school and improve!"*
took a course which, from the reality of the sight, was
likely to be beneficial: but every body is aware that
what is shewn at the theatres is nothing but an attempt to impose; and the audience rather sets itself
against the endeavour, than is impressed and corrected
by the moral. What, in the cant of the profession, is
called "illusion," we are satisfied, never exists; and
the actors are no more believed to be the characters
they represent, than the painted trees and castles of
the scenery are supposed to consist of rustling foliage
and substantial stone. Dr. Johnson says somewhere,
that the actor who for a moment could believe that
he was *Macbeth,* and really perpetrated the murders,
would deserve to be hanged; and, we may add, that
the audience would deserve it, too, as accessaries, for
not interfering on behalf of poor Duncan, if they were
persuaded that his life was in danger. We admire
a landscape for its truth, as a copy from nature, not
because we ever imagine that it is the actual view
itself, compressed into the compass of some three
feet of gilded frame: what we see on the stage is but
a succession of views with moving figures, and we
like them little or much in proportion as they approach

* Tom Brown's Works, vol. iv. 116.

our notions of reality; but always keeping the imitation perfectly distinct from the thing imitated, and approving the former only because it is an imitation.

"Live o'er each scene, and be what we behold,"

is a very good line from Pope; but if there be any "Roman virtue" in the British character, it does owe it to "Cato"; and it is remarkable, that it never was less apparent than at the time when that tragedy was oftenest represented: the littleness of party spirit was never more despicable, or more despicably displayed, than when "Cato" was first produced upon the stage.

As for the puppet-show of "Punch and Judy," it never is looked at, by the lowest of the populace, but as a mere joke; and a most effective part of that joke is the ultimate triumph of the hero: without it, the representation would be not only "flat and stale," but "unprofitable." We have seen it so; for we remember a showman, on one occasion, not merely receiving little or no money, but getting lamentably pelted with mud, because, from some scruple or other, he refused to allow the victory over the Devil to Punch. Besides, it may surely deserve consideration, whether, wicked as Punch unquestionably is, the Devil is not the worse offender of the two, and, consequently, the

more deserving of punishment. If so, poetical justice is satisfied.

We have before lamented that, as the performances
of Punch in this country very much resemble the impromptu comedies of the Italians, no record exists of the
dialogue, and, in few instances, of the course and series
of the scenery; the fact, most likely, being, that both
the one and the other were often altered to suit the
convenience of the manager, or the temper and wishes
of his auditory. We shall speak of some of these
variations presently; and in the mean time, and before
we lose sight of the connection between Don Juan
and the personage, who may now be justly called the
Don Juan of the multitude, we wish to add in this
place the only printed account we ever saw of the plot
of one of Punch's exhibitions, and which differs from
the story of any of the numerous shows we have
witnessed. It is given as a sort of theatrical criticism
in a letter from a watering-place, and was published
in the Morning Chronicle of 22nd September, 1813.
The narrative is as follows:

"Mr. Punch, a gentleman of great personal attraction, is married to Mrs. Judy, by whom he has a
lovely daughter, but to whom no name is given in this
piece, the infant being too young to be christened.
In a fit of horrid and demoniac jealousy, Mr. Punch,
like a second Zeluco, strangles his beauteous offspring.

Just as he has completed his dreadful purpose, Mrs. Judy enters, witnesses the brutal havoc, and *exit* screaming; she soon returns, however, armed with a bludgeon, and applies it to her husband's head, ' which to the wood returns a wooden sound.' Exasperated by jealousy and rage, Mr. Punch, at length, seizes another bludgeon, soon vanquishes his already weakened foe, and lays her prostrate at his feet; then, seizing the murdered infant and the expiring mother, he flings them both out of the window into the street. The dead bodies having been found, police officers enter the dwelling of Mr. Punch, who flies for his life, mounts his steed, and the author, neglecting, like other great poets, the confining unities of time and place, conveys his hero into Spain, where, however, he is arrested by an officer of the terrible Inquisition. After enduring the most cruel tortures with incredible fortitude, Mr. Punch, by means of a golden key (a beautiful and novel allegory), opens his prison door and escapes. The conclusion of the affecting story is satirical, allegorical, and poetical. The hero is first overtaken by weariness and laziness, in the shape of a black dog, whom he fights and conquers; disease, in the disguise of a physician, next arrests him; but Punch 'sees through the thin pretence,' and dismisses the doctor with a few derogatory kicks. Death at length visits the fugitive, but Punch lays about his skeleton carcase so lustily, and makes the bones of his antagonist rattle so musically with a *bastinado*, that 'Death his death's blow then received.' Last of all comes the Devil; first, under the appearance of a lovely female, but afterwards in his own natural shape, to drag the offender to the infernal regions, in purgatory to expiate his dreadful crimes. Even this attempt fails, and Punch is left triumphant over Doctors, Death and the Devil. The curtain falls amid the shouts of the Conqueror, who on his victorious staff lifts on high his vanquished foe."

We do not see, exactly, how the whole of such a plot could have been made out in a puppet-show, and we cannot avoid thinking, that this critic, like many others, has here found out "meanings never meant," and which could never have entered the head of any ordinary exhibitor.* With the exception of the skel-

---

* Casti, in his tale *La Pace di Pasquale* (Nov. xliii. vol. iii. Edit. 1804), mentions a friar who had *per le buffonerie raro talento,* and who was able, especially, *fare a maraviglia il Pulcinella.* M. D'Israeli also speaks of " a philosopher and a man of fortune," of his acquaintance, who delighted in performing "Punchinello's little comedy." We know several instances of fathers, who, for the amusement of their families, go through the part of the puppet-showman. These individuals might have sufficient invention for such a fable, but still it would not be easy to represent it intelligibly by puppets.

eton, all the other characters are familiar; and only supposing that the writer has a little disturbed the ordinary course of the events, for his own purpose of making out "more than meets the ear" in an allegory, the whole is very easily explained and understood.

The disregard of the unities of time and place is common to all the exhibitions of Punch we ever saw or have heard of, in this or any other country; and it may be the boast of Italy, that, while her regular drama wore these burdensome and useless fetters, under the patronage of the higher classes and the learned, they were thrown off in her *commedie à sogget-to,* under the patronage of the lower classes and the un-learned. It is not to be supposed, however, that in Italy the impromptu comedies, filled by the various charac-ters of Pulcinella, Harlequin, Scaramouch, the Doctor, and others, were exhibited only before the rabble of the community: the contrary might be satisfactorily es-tablished. The most dignified and the gravest not un-frequently laid aside their dignity and their gravity; and, like Leo X., rejoiced in the broadest repre-sentations of the buffoons.* Dr. Moore, who wrote

---

* " To such an extreme was this propensity carried, that his courtiers and attendants could not more effectually obtain his favour than by introducing to him such persons as, by their eccentricity, perversity, or imbecility of mind, were likely to

his "View of Italy," nearly fifty years ago, confesses
that he and the Duke of Hamilton, going to the performance with all possible prejudices against it, were
delighted: he especially dwells upon a most ludicrous
scene, in which Harlequin made a stammerer bring
out a word which had been sticking in his throat for
a quarter of an hour, by striking him on the back, as
nurses strike a choking infant.* Recently, we have
seen a refined French auditory laugh heartily at the
very same incident, the only difference being, that
Potier was not dressed as Harlequin, nor Brunet as
Pulcinella.

At various periods, the adventures of Punch have
been differently represented and misrepresented, and
innovations have been introduced, to suit the taste
and to meet the events of the day. One attempt of
this sort was made in Fielding's time, in consequence
of the extreme popularity of "the Provoked Husband." He complains ("Tom Jones," Book xii.

excite his mirth." Roscoe's Leo X. iv. 370, Edit. 1827. This
author is at a difficulty to account for this "propensity,"
which is easily explained on the principle of contrast. It is
fortunate for his gravity that *Punch and Judy* were not invented in the time of Leo, for the Pope would certainly have kept
a puppet-show for his own private amusement.

* Vol. i. p. 258.

chap. 5) that a puppet-show, witnessed by his hero,
included "the fine and serious part" of the comedy
we have named. He then proceeds, from the mouth
of Jones, to shew its inferiority to the old exhibition
of Punch and his wife (whom he miscalls *Joan*, by
some strange forgetfulness, although her name has
been *Judy*, as the lawyers say, "from time whereof
the memory of man runneth not to the contrary"),
which gives some offence to "the dancer of wires,"
who fancied, as he might do very reasonably, that
"people rose from his little drama as much improved
as they could do from the great."

Of later years, we have witnessed several singular
interpolations. After the battle of the Nile, Lord Nelson figured on one of the street-stages, and held a
dialogue with Punch, in which he endeavoured to
persuade him, as a brave fellow, to go on board his
ship, and assist in fighting the French: "Come,
Punch, my boy (said the naval hero), I'll make you
a captain or a commodore, if you like it."—"But I
don't like it (replied the puppet-show hero); I shall
be drowned." — "Never fear that (answered Nelson); he that is born to be hanged, you know, is
sure not to be drowned." During one of the Elections
for Westminster, Sir F. Burdett received equal hon-
our, and was represented kissing Judy and the child,

and soliciting Mr. Punch for his vote. "How are you,
Mr. Punch? (enquired the Baronet), I hope you will
give me your support."—"I don't know (answered
Punch), ask my wife. I leave all those things to Mrs.
P."—"That is very right (continued Sir Francis),
what do you say, Mrs. Judy? Bless me! what a sweet
little child you have got, I wish mine were like it."—
"And so they may be, Sir Francis (observed Judy),
for you are very like my husband; you have got such
a beautiful long nose."—"True, Mrs. Judy; but Lady
B. is not like you (added Sir Francis, kissing her).
A sweet little infant, indeed! I hope it has good
health. How are its little bowels?"—"Charmingly,
thank you," was the answer; and Judy could not refuse the solicitations of so gallant and kind hearted a
candidate.

At a country fair, we once saw a donkey-race represented by puppets with a great deal of spirit, and
we need hardly add, that Mr. Punch* (though not
always the most expert horseman) rode the winner,
but was cheated out of the prize. It is not uncommon
now, among the showmen *in eyre*, to insert a scene of
a street-row: for this purpose they introduce a watch-

* See Act ii. Sc. 2. of the "Tragical Comedy of Punch and
Judy," where the hero is thrown by his horse, Hector.

box with a *Charley* in it, fast asleep. Punch enters
tipsey, over turns the "guardian of the night," and,
finally, is taken to the watch-house. This incident is
of "Tom and Jerry" origin, and was not used until
those heroes figured in the pages of *Life in London.*
Within the last twenty years, at various times, we
have observed characters inserted from popular performances at our theatres : some of our readers may
recollect a conference between Blue Beard and
Punch, on the mutually interesting topic of a plu-
rality of wives; and Morgiana from *The Forty Thieves,*
and Grimaldi from *Mother Goose,* have danced together before us. While this work has been in a course
of preparation, we had the satisfaction of being present at an interview between Punch and a person no
less distinguished than Paul Pry, in which the latter
received severe chastisement for "intruding," while
the former was enjoying the delightful converse of
one of his female acquaintances.

CHAPTER VI.

ON THE CHARACTER OF PUNCH.

PROFESSOR Richardson, of Glasgow, as every body
knows, wrote a series of "Essays on Shakspeare's
Dramatic Characters," in which he entered at length
into the design of the author, and the manner in which
he had accomplished it. Other admirers of the works
of the same poet have published separate dissertations
on particular personages in his plays, such as Falstaff,
Hamlet, &c. It seems to us, that Punch, although
not drawn by the same "master-hand," merits a similar distinction; and we shall accordingly proceed to
offer a few remarks upon his character, as it is displayed in the most approved representations of the
present day. Professor Richardson declared, even in
his "fifth edition," that "his work was unworthy of

* Published in 1797. We believe there are several later
impressions.

the public notice" (rather a bad compliment to his many readers), while we, on the contrary, in our first impression, contend that our remarks well deserve attention; and we shall "be of the same opinion still," even if "convinced, against our will," that our work will never arrive at an equal degree of popularity.

We are more disposed to offer a few observations on the character of Punch, because upon none of the *dramatis personæ* of Shakspeare's plays has Professor Richardson bestowed a larger space, or a greater degree of labour, than on Richard III. and Sir John Falstaff: to both of these is Punch, in disposition and talents, akin; and he, besides, combines in his own person the deformity of the one* and the obesity

---

*As he was to have "a spice or somewhat more" of Don Juan about him, and as we are told

"A decent leg is what all ladies like,"

it was not thought expedient, by the inventor or inventors of Punch, to represent him with Richard's tibial disfigurement. Punch's legs are not "legs for boots," but legs fit "to make legs with," and to make legs by. We never saw him at any exhibition without a pair, models of their kind, and in shewing which he evinced no slight degree of vanity. There is not, at present, such a thing as a good male leg on the stage; so that Punch may be excused if he is a little ostentatious. Lord Byron calls a delicate hand and a good leg the

of the other. He is, as it were, a combination and
concentration of two of the most prominent and original delineations on the stage: as if

"The force of nature could no farther go:
To make a third, she joined the other two."

The similarity between Richard and Falstaff, though
not very obvious, has been fully established; and it
consists in the intellectual superiority they both possess, and with the exercise of which the first gratifies
his ambition, and the last his appetites. It is the
possession of the same high talents (in the last instance applied very much to the attainment of the
same ends) which constitutes Punch's chief moral resemblance. The high authority to which we have just
alluded lays it down, and, we may say, proves that
"the pleasure we receive from the character of
Richard is produced by those emotions which arise
in the mind, on beholding great intellectual ability
employed for inhuman and perfidious purposes."* If
we try the character of Punch by this test, shall

criterion of good blood; Punch's leg is not so remarkable for
"a vulgar quantity of calf," as for the fineness of its ankle,
and the general symmetry of its proportions.
*Edit. 1797, p. 204.

we not arrive at the identical conclusion? Like the
"crook-back prodigy," he is not "shaped for sportive
tricks," and

"wants love's majesty,
To strut before a wanton, ambling nymph:"

but to compensate for these personal defects, Punch,
like Richard, has "a tongue shall wheedle with the
Devil," and he does, in fact, "wheedle with the Devil,"
to some purpose. His wit, his ingenuity, his rapid invention of expedients, or, in two words, his "intellectual ability," is employed for "inhuman and perfidious purposes," and hence the delight we experience
during the representation of those scenes in which his
genius is displayed.* We freely admit that, as far as
the moral is concerned, Shakspeare has the advantage
of the author of "Punch and Judy," in both instances:

---

* We have elsewhere alluded to the possible intentions of
Silvio Fiorillo in giving Punch such a stupendous nose; but
we omitted one reason which may here be assigned, and would
have been the more applicable, had our hero in Italy at all times
possessed the same unrivalled talents he invariably displays in
this country. This reason is contained in the productions of
some of the Burlesque Poets of Italy; who, however, as we have
before remarked, do not, and could not, mention Punch, as he
was not invented when they most flourished. Ludovico Dolce
has a *capitolo in lode del Naso,* highly extolling *un gran pezzo di
naso,* and declaring *che l huomo è degno d'ogni stima* who is so

Richard is slain, and Falstaff dismissed with contempt; but to this point we have already adverted in the preceding chapter.

"The desire of gratifying the grosser and lower appetites is the ruling and strongest principle in the mind of Falstaff."* Only substitute the name of Punch for that of the fat, witty, and luxurious knight, and every syllable is equally applicable. A great deal has been written *pro* and *con*, on the question of Falstaff's

provided: he afterwards proceeds thus in point, and that point is not lost in our translation.

> If any man has but a gracious nose,
>   I mean a nose in longitude not scanty,
> His brain with wit and fancy overflows.
>
>   Do we not know that the immortal Dante
> Had a huge nose? and that's the real cause
>   He wrote so well.—Ovid, in style so janty,
>
> And yet so natural, obtain'd applause
>   By his great nose, which likewise gave him name:
> Horace and Virgil envied him.—His jaws
>
>   Berni had vainly open'd, to his shame,
> And to the loss of our supreme delight,
>   But that his nose was like a torch on flame.

Punch has a similar ornament, and the same causes produce the same effects.

* Richardson's, Essays 1797, p. 249.

cowardice, and it now seems agreed by the learned, not "the commentators on Shakspeare,"

"Deep-vers'd in books and shallow in themselves;
   Crude and intoxicate, collecting toys
   And trifles for choice matters, worth a sponge:"

but, by those who have some knowledge of the human mind and its operations, that Falstaff is no coward: while he avows "discretion to be the better part of valour," he only avoids situations of danger, not from constitutional fear of them, but because his strong sense revolts at incurring peril where it is needless. As one of our old translators of Horace shrewdly says, in reference to that poet's disappearance at the battle of Philippi, "a soldier is no more bound to fight when he is out of his humour, than an orator to speak when he is out of his wits; nor is it prudent for a man of wit and learning to have his brains beaten out by one that has none."* Such is precisely the "discretion," which Falstaff commends. Punch, however, is less prudent than Falstaff, and, in some instances, may, perhaps, be almost charged with being a little fool-hardy. He is more amorous; and in

---

* Alexander Broome's "Life of Horace," prefixed to "The Poems of Horace," &c., "by several hands." London, 1666.

seeking to gratify this propensity, he must, of course, be sometimes prepared, like Don Juan (whom in this respect he resembles), "to run upon the very edge of hazard." If, in the course of his adventures, Punch be now and then guilty of ridiculous extravagancies, apparently inconsistent with part of the character we have drawn of him, let it be remembered in the words of Pascal, "*l'extreme esprit est accusée de la folie, comme l'extreme défaut.*"

We have it upon very high and ancient authority, that "no bad man can be happy,"* and, if this maxim be true, the character of Punch is so far out of nature: he hardly knows a moment's unhappiness, from the beginning to the end of his career, scarcely excepting even the period of his confinement before he is led out to execution. Punch, in this respect, beats Macheath, as they used to say, "out of all cry;" but then the Captain, compared with Punch, is only a "petty-larceny villain," who is obliged to dose himself with brandy. Punch's confidence and presence of mind never desert him; and these qualities, combined with his personal, but prudent, courage, carry him through every difficulty, and enable him to triumph over every adversary. The great French satirist severely lashes those writers, who

* Nemo malus fœlix, &c. Juv. Sat. iv.

"make vice amiable";* and of this charge, we cannot acquit the author or authors of "Punch and Judy." In the person of the hero, and in the success of his criminal attempts, vice is most assuredly rendered too attractive, if we suppose that his example can have any effect upon those who witness his amusing performances.

Such is the character of Punch, as he is represented in this country, but in Italy he still preserves most of the qualities for which he was originally notorious. Baretti tells us, that his part is that of a "timid weak fellow, who is always thrashed by the other actors, and always boasts of victory after they are gone";† and the author of a modern work, upon the manners and amusements of the Italians, thus speaks of the exhibitions in which Punch is engaged and of the figure he cuts in them.

"Two inferior theatres, La Fenice and San Carlino, both in the Largo del Castello, are chiefly devoted to farces and pantomimes. There you see Policinella in his genuine colours. Policinella is represented as a

---

* Je ne puis estimer ces dangereux auteurs
   Qui, de l'honneur en vers infames déserteurs,
   Trahissent la vertu sur un papier coupable,
   Aux yeux de leurs lecteurs rendent le vice aimable.
                Boileau Art. Poet. ch. iv.
† Tolondron, p. 324.

servant of Acerra,* a village in the neighbourhood of Naples, and he is so highly gifted by nature and accomplished by education, that he is at once a thief, a liar, a coward, a braggart, and a debauchee: still the facetious way in which he relates his various feats, enraptures the grovelling countrymen. He delights in licentious *double entendre*, gross jokes, and dirty tricks; there is not a single good quality in him: his cunning is very low, and he is always outwitted when he meets with any person of sense, so that in the end he is generally discovered, imprisoned, whipped, and hanged. Such is the celebrated Policinella. There are many houses for puppet-shows, where, at any time of the day, one may go in for a few *grains*, provided one's olfactory nerves are not too keen for the smell produced by the crowd of dirty fellows who resort to them. There are also ambulatory puppet-shows in the streets." †

* See chap. i. of this work.

† "Italy, and the Italians in the Nineteenth Century," chap. i. The dress worn by Punch is represented in one of Penelli's *Cinquanta Costumi Pittoreschi*, Rome, 1816. It represents the performance of a puppet-show in the streets of Rome, exactly in the same way as they are exhibited in this country. In Naples, sometimes a third person stands on an elevation at the side, and explains, or *interprets*, for the characters. Penelli makes Punch wear a black mask, like Harlequin.

It has been said, that " in England every thing intellectual advances by rapid strides ; " and no more
striking or convincing proof can be given of its truth
than the change, especially of late years, which has
occurred in the character of Punch. In Italy, he has remained stationary : he is there now, what he was two
hundred years ago ; but here, he is no longer the blunt-
headed booby, " always outwitted," represented in the
preceding extract, but a personage in general far too
clever for any of those with whom he has to deal :
instead of being " discovered " and " hanged," he con-
trives to have his executioner " trussed up " in his
place ; and finally, by the happy union of intellect and
corporeal strength, defeats and destroys " man's greatest enemy," and becomes " the devil's butcher," when
the fiend hoped to have had him " in fee simple, with
fine and recovery."

We cannot close the character of our hero without
inserting a sonnet (and its *coda*, as the Italians call
it) in praise of Punch, by no less a man, if we
are rightly informed, than the poet, among whose
latest works it was to continue and vary the story of
" Don Juan." It is highly characteristic of the author,
and of the representation it celebrates with so much
truth and vivacity.

SONNET TO PUNCH.

Triumphant Punch! with joy I follow thee
 Thro' the glad progress of thy wanton course;
 Where life is painted with such truth and force,
Its equal on our stage we never see.
Whether thou kill'st thy wife with jolly glee,
 Hurl'st thy sweet babe away without remorse,
 Mount'st, and art quickly thrown from off thy horse,
Or dance with "pretty Poll," so fair and free;
 Having first slain with just disdain her sire,
 Deaf to music of thy sheep-bell lyre:
Who loves not music, is not fit to live!
 Then, when the hangman comes, who can refuse
 To laugh, when thou his head into the noose
Hast nimbly thrust, while he gets no reprieve?
        Who feigns to grieve
Thou goest unpunish'd in the fiend's despite,
And slay'st him too, is but a hypocrite.
         'Tis such delight
To see thee cudgel his black carcase antique,
For very rapture I am almost frantic!

Having now traced the history of Mr. Punch,* we
shall proceed, we believe, for the first time in this or
any other country, to put his performances upon record.

* In reference to the origin of his family name, we may add,
that some have erroneously derived it from the liquor *punch*
(which itself comes from the Indian *Palepuntz*, or *Palepunsche*),
on the same principle that the Italian character Macaroni is

It is time to do so for the benefit of posterity; lest, as society gradually acquires a more superfine polish than it even now possesses, it should be impossible, hereafter, to print what is fortunately yet considered innocent and harmless. Addison tells us, that "the merry people of the world are the amiable," and in the language of "a man forbid," we address ourselves to those,

> *Chi amano, senza smorfia e ipocrisia,*
> *Gl' innocenti piaceri e l'allegria.*

---

said to have been taken from the approved dish of that name and as our Jack Pudding and the German *Hanns Wurst* (before mentioned), from the attachment of the mob to puddings or sausages. The fact is, that *Punch* is only a familiar abbreviation of *Punchinello,* which is itself corrupted from *Pulcinella.*

THE

TRAGICAL COMEDY, OR COMICAL TRAGEDY,

OF

PUNCH AND JUDY.

PREFACE.

THE following drama is founded chiefly upon the performance of an old Italian way-faring puppet-show-man of the name of Piccini, who has perambulated town and country for the last forty or fifty years. Like the representations of our early stage, it was not by him distinguished into acts and scenes, but the divisions were easily made; and the whole now assumes a shape, in which it may rival most of the theatrical productions of the present day, whether by Poole, popular for his *Paul Pry*, Peake for his puns, Planché for his poetry, Peacock for his parodies, or Payne for his plagiarisms.

Piccini lives in the classical vicinity of Drury Lane, and is now infirm; but he still travels about, considering it "no sin to labour in his vocation": he is thus described by a writer in a discontinued periodi-

cal, called the *Literary Speculum,* which we quote, because it is the only printed notice we have seen of an
individual so generally known. It is to be observed,
that the article to which we are indebted, was published seven years ago, and the author of it speaks of his
own youth, when Piccini's age was "as a lusty winter,
frosty but kindly," and before "time, the old clock-set-
ter," had nearly let him run the whole length of his chain
without winding him up again. "He (Piccini) was
an Italian; a little thick-set man, with a red humorous looking countenance. He had lost one eye, but
the other made up for the absence of its fellow by a
shrewdness of expression sufficient for both. He
always wore an oil-skin hat and a rough great coat.
At his back he carried a deal box, containing the *dramatis personæ* of his little theatre; and in his hand
the trumpet, at whose glad summons, hundreds of
merry laughter-loving faces flocked round him with
gaping mouths and anxious looks, all eager to renew
their acquaintance with their old friend and favourite,
Punch. The theatre itself was carried by a tall man,
who seemed a sort of sleeping partner in the concern,
or mere *dumb-waiter* on the other's operations." The
wood-cut on our title-page, precisely corresponds
with this lively description, making some allowance
for the difference of age in the master of the puppet-

show; still, however, not too old to carry his deal box and to blow "an inspiring air."

Besides Piccini's representation, we have compared the following pages with, and corrected them by the exhibitions of other perambulatory *artistes* (as our neighbours term them), now flourishing, or who have done so during the last fifteen or twenty years. It will be remarked that various parodies and snatches of songs are introduced, which are at present commonly omitted, though adding greatly to the humour and spirit of the piece: for many of these we are indebted to a manuscript, with the use of which we have been favoured by a gentleman who undertook, about the year 1796, to perform the task we have now executed, by giving the unwritten, if not strictly *extempore*, dialogue of "Punch and Judy" a permanent and tangible shape. The tunes and the words for these musical accompaniments of the puppet-show have varied from time to time, according to circumstances; they take a tolerably extensive range, the oldest being adapted from *The Beggars' Opera*, first acted exactly one hundred years ago, and the most modern from *Guy Mannering*.

Piccini's exhibition was, in the first instance, purely Italian, and such colloquies as he introduced were in the language of that country: he soon learnt a little broken English, and adapted his shew more to the taste of English audiences. It is too much to suppose that the notion that Punch is a foreigner, and ought always to speak like one, is taken from Piccini, because Punch has been looked upon as a stranger more welcome than most, from the first moment he set his foot in this country. The performers of "Punch and Judy," who are natives of Great Britain, generally endeavour to imitate an "outlandish dialect."

There is one peculiarity about Piccini's puppets which deserves notice: they are much better carved, the features having a more marked and comic expression, than those of his rivals. He brought most of them over with him from Italy, and he complains that in England he had not been able to find any workman capable of adequately supplying the loss, if by chance one of his figures has been broken or stolen. Why his Punch has also been made to squint, or at least to have what is known by the epithet of a swivel-eye, unless for the sake of humour, or distinction, does not appear: in this obliquity of vision he only follows the greatest hero of Italian romance, Orlando, of whom Pulci tells us,

> *Orlando molto ne gli occhi era fiero;*
> *Tanto che alcun autore dice e pone,*
> *Ch' egli era un poco guercio, a dire il vero.*

These lines are in Canto xx. of the *Morgante Maggiore:* in the following Canto he repeats the assertion, in which he is supported by Boiardo in various parts of his *Orlando Innamorato,* but particularly in Canto xli., where Astolpho in high indignation against the Paladin, exclaims,

> —— *Ov' è quel guercio traditore,*
> *Ch' ha tanto ardir di dir ch' io son buffone?*

In fact, Orlando, as drawn by these poets, had little but his strength and courage to make the ladies love him, and the Pagans fear him; and in all respects he was far inferior to Punch.

We have already spoken of Le Sage and Piron, as writers of puppet-plays, and we might have introduced many other distinguished authors who lived about the opening of the last century. It is well known how popular this species of entertainment was, and still is in Germany; and its dignity will receive a considerable accession, from the fact, that the greatest poet of that country, Goëthe, did not scruple to write one on the sacred story of Esther and Ahasuerus: he calls it *Neueröffnetes moralisch-politisches Puppenspiel,* and *Hanns Wurst,* or Jack Pudding, is employed to amuse the spectators between the acts.

DRAMATIS PERSONÆ.

PUNCH.

SCARAMOUCH.

THE CHILD.

COURTIER.

DOCTOR.

SERVANT.

BLIND MAN.

CONSTABLE.

POLICE OFFICER.

JACK KETCH.

THE DEVIL.

TOBY.

HECTOR.

JUDY.

POLLY.

THE
TRAGICAL COMEDY, OR COMICAL TRAGEDY,
OF
PUNCH AND JUDY.

ENTER PUNCH.

After a few preliminary squeaks, he bows three times
to the spectators;—once in the centre, and once at
each side of the stage, and then speaks the following

PROLOGUE.*

Ladies and Gentlemen, pray how you do?
If you all happy, me all happy too.
Stop and hear my merry littel play;
If me make you laugh, me need not make you pay.

[*Exit.*

---

* The ancient *motions*, or puppet-shows, had prologues, as
appears, among other authorities, from Jasper Mayne's *City
March*, Act v. Sc. 2.

——— "like a buskin'd prologue, in
A stately, high, majestic *motion*, bare."

Powell also, as we have already seen (vide Chap. iii), attacked

ACT I.—SCENE I.

Punch is heard behind the scene, squeaking the tune of *Malbroug s'en vat en guerre:* * he then makes his appearance and dances about the stage, while he sings to the same air,

> ·   Mr. Punch is one jolly good fellow,
> His dress is all scarlet and yellow, †
> And if now and then he gets mellow,
>   It's only among his good friends.
>   His money most freely he spends;
>   To laugh and grow fat he intends;
> With the girls he's a rogue and a rover;
> ·   He lives, while he can, upon clover;
> When he dies—it's only all over;
>   And there Punch's comedy ends.

Isaac Bickerstaff, Esq., in a prologue. Puppet-showmen, now-adays, seem to have adopted Cumberland's opinion, in his *Observer*, that prologues and epilogues are useless appendages.

* This air and the Marseilles March, afterwards spoken of, were popular nearly forty years ago, and doubtless were then first introduced, as substitutes for others which had become less acceptable. Very recently the tune of *Malbroug* has again come into vogue with the lower orders.

† Scarlet and yellow are still proverbially called "Tom Fool's colours," which may form another slight link of connexion between Punch and the clown of our old comedies, and the court jesters of our ancestors.

He continues to dance and sing, and then calls "Judy, my dear! Judy!"

ENTER THE DOG TOBY.

Punch. Hollo, Toby! who call'd you? How you do, Mr. Toby? Hope you very well, Mr. Toby.

Toby. Bow, wow, wow!

Punch. How do my good friend, your master, Mr. Toby? How do Mr. Scaramouch?*

Toby. Bow, wow, wow!

Punch. I'm glad to hear it.—Poor Toby! What a nice good-temper'd dog it is! No wonder his master is so fond of him.

---

* The Italian character in the impromptu comedies, called *Scaramouch*, was known in England, and considerably before *Pulcinella* made his appearance. He gives the title to Ravenscroft's comedy, and in Durfey's *Madame Fickle*, licenced in 1676, Toby, the son of Mr. Tilbery, is made to employ it as a fashionable term of abuse, "*Scaramouchi*, Rascal, Poltron, Popinjay!—Son of twenty fathers!" &c. Act ii. Soon after the year 1720, Punch became a common character in afterpieces. —In the "Weekly Journal" of Dec. 14, 1723, the plot of *Harlequin and Dr. Faustus* is given, in which it appears that Punch performed the part of one of the Doctor's scholars. Duplessis was a celebrated Punch, and performed for Chetwood's benefit, in 1726.

Toby. [Snarls.] Arr! Arr!*

Punch. What! Toby! you cross this morning? You get out of bed the wrong way upwards?

Toby. [Snarls again.] Arr! Arr!

Punch. Poor Toby. [Putting his hand out cautiously, and trying to coax the dog, who snaps at it.] Toby, you're one nasty cross dog: get away with you! [Strikes at him.]

Toby. Bow, wow, wow! [Seizing Punch by the nose.]

Punch. Oh, dear! Oh, dear! My nose! my poor nose! my beautiful nose! Get away! get away, you nasty dog —I tell your master. Oh, dear! dear!— Judy! Judy!

[Punch shakes his nose, but cannot shake off the dog, who follows him as he retreats round the stage. He continues to call "Judy! Judy, my dear!" until the dog quits its hold, and *exit.*]

Punch. [*Solus,* and rubbing his nose with both hands.] Oh, my nose! my pretty littel nose!† Judy!

---

* In reference to this sound, Shakspeare tells us that "R is the dog's letter." *Rom. and Jul.* Act ii. Scene 5.

† Punch's nose, which he here calls "little," ironically, according to the authority of one of our old play-wrights, would lead us to conclude him rather of Florentine than of Neapolitan origin. —Lod. Barry, in his laughable comedy of

Judy! You nasty, nasty brute, I will tell you master of you. Mr. Scaramouch! [Calls.] My good friend, Mr. Scaramouch! Look what you nasty brute dog has done!

manners, called *Ram Alley*, printed in 1611, and reprinted in the new edition of *Dodsley's Old Plays*, vol. v. has a curious and humorous passage on the diversity of noses, a part of which only is here applicable, but we shall be pardoned for quoting the whole.

—————— " I'll tell thee what
A witty woman may with ease distinguish
All men by their noses, as thus : your nose
Tuscan is lovely, large, and broad,
Much like a goose ; your valiant generous nose,
A crooked, smooth, and a great puffing nose.
Your scholar's nose is very fresh and raw,
For want of fire in winter, and quickly smells
His chops of mutton in his dish of porage.
Your puritan nose is very sharp and long,
And much like your widow's, and with ease can smell
An edifying capon five streets off."

This dissertation is worthy of Slaukenbergius. The nose of our hero is " lovely, large, and broad," like " your nose Tuscan," and it is at the same time a

" valiant generous nose,
A crooked, smooth, and a great puffing nose."

SCENE II.

ENTER SCARAMOUCH — *with a stick.*

Scaramouch. Hollo! Mr. Punch! What have you been doing to my poor dog?

Punch. [Retreating behind the side scene, on observing the stick, and peeping round the corner.] Ha! my good friend! how you do? glad to see you look so well. [*Aside.*] I wish you were farther with your nasty great stick.

Scaramouch. You have been beating and ill-using my poor dog, Mr. Punch.

Punch. He has been biting and ill-using my poor nose.—What have you got there, sir?

Scaramouch. Where?

Punch. In your hand?

Scaramouch. A fiddle.

Punch. A fiddel! what a pretty thing is a fiddel! Can you play upon that fiddel?

Scaramouch. Come here, and I'll try.

Punch. No, thank you—I can hear the music here, very well.

Scaramouch. Then you shall try yourself. Can you play?

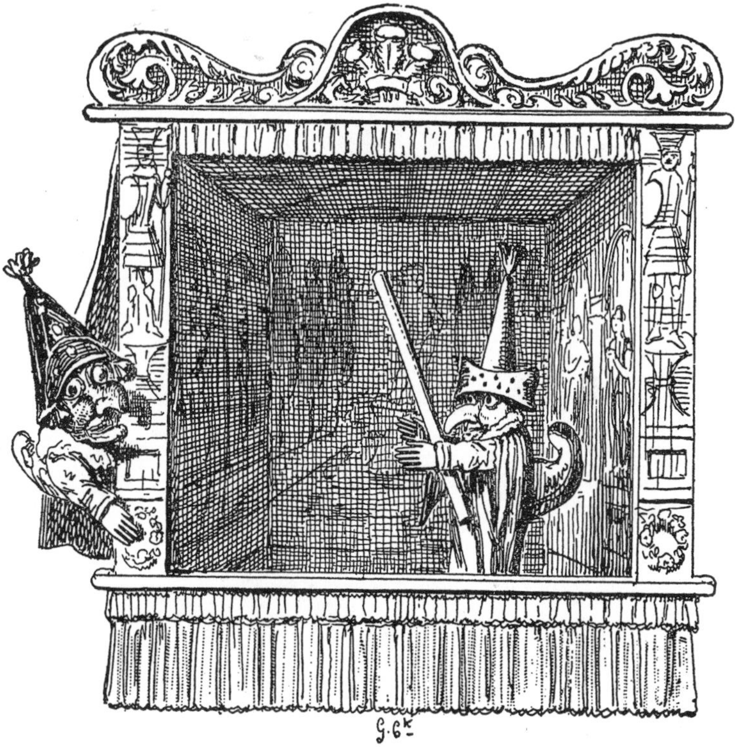
G. Ck

Punch. [Coming in.] I do not know, till I try.*
Let me see! [Takes the stick, and moves slowly
about, singing the tune of the *Marche des Marseillois.*
He hits Scaramouch a slight blow on his high cap, as
if by accident.]

Scaramouch. You play very well, Mr. Punch. Now,
let me try. I will give you a lesson how to play the
fiddle. [Takes the stick, and dances to the same
tune, hitting Punch a hard blow on the back of his
head.] There's sweet music for you.

Punch. I no like you playing so well as my own.
Let me again. [Takes the stick, and dances as before: in the course of his dance he gets behind Scaramouch, and, with a violent blow, knocks his head clean
off his shoulders.] How you like that tune, my good
friend? That sweet music, or sour music, eh?† He!

---

* This is a regular "Joe, p. 47." Every body must remember Mr. Miller's story of the countryman, who was asked if he
could play upon the violin, and who answered that he "did
not know, because, as how, he had never tried." There may,
however, be some corresponding joke in Italian. We have
read it in French.

† "How sour sweet music is, when *time* is broke."

Richard II. Act v. Scene 5.

Substitute *head* for *time*, and the line would be very applicable.
Had Punch meant any allusion to it, he would have made the
quotation and the change.

he! he! [Laughing, and throwing away the stick.]
You'll never hear such another tune, so long as you
live, my boy. [Sings the tune of "*Malbroug*," and
dances to it.] Judy! Judy, my dear! Judy! can't you
answer, my dear?

Judy. [Within.] Well! what do you want, Mr.
Punch?

Punch. Come up stairs: I want you.

Judy. Then want must be your master. I'm busy.

Punch. [Singing, tune "*Malbroug.*"]

> Her answer genteel is and civil!
> No wonder, you think, if we live ill,
> And I wish her sometimes at the Devil,
> Since that's all the answer I get.
> Yet, why should I grumble and fret,
> Because she's sometimes in a pet?
> Though I really am sorry to say, Sirs,
> That that is too often her way, Sirs.
> For this, by and by, she shall pay, Sirs.
> Oh, wives are an obstinate set!

Judy, my dear! [Calling.] Judy, my love! pretty
Judy! come up stairs.

SCENE III.

ENTER JUDY.

Judy. Well, here I am! what do you want, now I'm come?

Punch. [Aside.] What a pretty creature! An't she one beauty?

Judy. What do you want, I say?

Punch. A kiss! a pretty kiss! [Kisses her, while she hits him a slap on the face.]

Judy. Take that then: how do you like my kisses? Will you have another?

Punch. No; one at a time, one at a time, my sweet pretty wife. [Aside.] She always is so playful.—Where's the child? Fetch me the child, Judy, my dear.

[*Exit* Judy.

Punch. [*Solus.*] There's one wife for you! What a precious darling creature? She go to fetch our child.*

---

* The MS. to which we are very much indebted for the musical department of our drama, supplies another stanza to the tune of *Malbroug,* which we have excluded from the text, as it contains already two specimens of the kind, and the simile regarding her voice is used afterwards. It is, however, worth adding in a note. Punch sings it after he has received the slap on the face, and while Judy is gone for the child:

RE-ENTER JUDY WITH THE CHILD.

Judy. Here's the child. Pretty dear! It knows its papa. Take the child.

Punch. [Holding out his hands.] Give it me—pretty littel thing! How like its sweet mamma!

Judy. How awkward you are!

Punch. Give it me: I know how to nurse it so well as you do. [She gives it him.] Get away! [*Exit* Judy. Punch nursing the child in his arms.] What a pretty baby it is! was it sleepy then? Hush-a-by, by, by.— [Sings to the tune of "*Rest thee, babe.*"*]

> Oh, rest thee, my baby,
>   Thy daddy is here:
> Thy mammy's a gaby,
>   And that's very clear.

> My wife is a beautiful darling,
> And though her tongue goes like a starling,
> We seldom have fighting or snarling:
>   Her voice is delightful to hear!
>   But take care you don't get too near;
>   Sometimes her behaviour is queer:
> With her hands she has always been handy.
> I must doctor my face with some brandy,
> And sweetened with white sugar-candy,
>   I'll take it inside, never fear.

* Evidently an interpolation since *Guy Mannering* was

Oh, rest thee, my darling,
Thy mother will come,
With voice like a starling;—
I wish she was dumb!

Poor dear littel thing! it cannot get to sleep: by, by; by, by, hush-a-by. Well, then, it shan't. [Dances the child, and then sets it on his lap, between his knees, and sings the common nursery ditty,]

Dancy baby diddy;
What shall daddy do widdy?
Sit on his lap,
Give it some pap;
Dancy baby diddy. *

[After nursing it upon his lap, Punch sticks the child against the side of the stage, on the platform, and

brought upon the stage. For what song this parody was substituted, cannot now be ascertained.

* The admirers of "the antiquities of nursery literature" (to use the words of the *Quarterly Review*, which wisely devoted some sheets to the subject) may like to see a different version of this "delicate and simple ditty," which we have on the highest authority. It runs thus:

"Dancy, baby, dancy,
How it shall gallop and prancy!
Sit on my knee;
Now kissy me:
Dancy, baby, dancy."

going himself to the opposite side, runs up to it, clapping his hands, and crying, "Catchee, catchee, catchee!" He then takes it up again, and it begins to cry.]

What is the matter with it. Poor thing! It has got the stomach ache, I dare say. [Child cries.] Hush-a-by, hush-a-by! [Sitting down, and rolling it on his knees.] Naughty child!—Judy! [Calling.] the child has got the stomach-ache. Pheu! Nasty child! Judy, I say! [Child continues to cry.] Keep quiet, can't you? [Hits it a box on the ear.] Oh, you filthy child! What have you done? I won't keep such a nasty child. Hold your tongue! [Strikes the child's head several times against the side of the stage.] There!—there!—there! How you like that? I thought I stop your squalling. Get along with you, nasty, naughty, crying child. [Throws it over the front of the stage among the spectators.]—He! he! he! [Laughing and singing to the same tune as before.]

> Get away, nasty baby;
> There it goes over:
> Thy mammy's a gaby,
> Thy daddy's a rover.

RE-ENTER JUDY.

Judy. Where is the child?

Punch. Gone,—gone to sleep.*

Judy. What have you done with the child, I say?

Punch. Gone to sleep, I say.

Judy. What have you done with it?

Punch. What have I done with it?

Judy. Ay; done with it!† I heard it crying just now. Where is it?

Punch. How should I know?

Judy. I heard you make the pretty darling cry.

Punch. I dropped it out at window.

Judy. Oh, you cruel horrid wretch, to drop the pretty baby out at window. Oh! [Cries and wipes her eyes with the corner of her white apron.] You barbarous man. Oh!

Punch. You shall have one other soon, Judy, my dear. More where that come from.‡

---

* Punch equivocates between death itself and the "ape of death."

> "After life's fitful fever it *sleeps* well."
>
> *Macbeth*, Act iii. Scene 2.

† Judy might say with the Moor—

> Done with it?—"By heaven, he echoes me,
>   As if there were some monster in his thought
>   Too hideous to be shewn."   *Othello*, Act iii. Sc. 3.

‡ This may remind the reader of an anecdote in Machiavelli's *Discorsi* (Lib. iii. cap. 6, *Delle Congiurie*) where Caterina,

Judy. I'll make you pay for this, depend upon it.

[*Exit* in haste.

Punch. There she goes. What a piece of work about nothing!* [Dances about and sings, beating time with his head, as he turns round, on the front of the stage.]

RE-ENTER JUDY, with a stick. She comes in behind, and hits Punch a sounding blow on the back of the head, before he is aware.

Judy. I'll teach you to drop my child out at window.

the wife of Girolamo Riario, Count of Forli, in a very extraordinary manner, defied her enemies, and shewed how little she valued the lives of her sons. — Mr. Roscoe (Life of Lorenzo de' Medici, ii. 164, edit. 1825) does not seem to be aware that the story is to be found in Machiavelli, and he quotes Muratori's *Annals,* ix. 556, for his authority. Muratori treats the point with great decorum: *Rispose loro quella forte femmina, che se avessero fatti perir que' figliuoli, restavano a lei le forme per farne de gli altri.*

* "This nothing's more than matter," and yet Punch was right in the sense in which Shakspeare speaks in *Coriolanus :*

" It was a thing of nothing — *titleless,*"

for the infant has no name, and it is uncertain whether it ever was christened. We have heard it invariably spoken of as

Punch. So-o-oftly, Judy, so-o-oftly! [Rubbing the back of his head with his hand.] Don't be a fool now.* What you at ?

Judy. What! you'll drop my poor baby out at window again, will you? [Hitting him continually on the head.]

Punch. No, I never will again. [She still hits him.] Softly, I say, softly. A joke's a joke!

" the child "; and even its sex is doubtful, unless we take the word of Thomson, "Heroes are sires of boys," and then we shall, of course, conclude that Punch's offspring was a man-child.

* This was the great Grimaldi's celebrated exclamation in *Mother Goose* and elsewhere, and from him it seems borrowed : we call him "the great Grimaldi" to distinguish him from his great grand-father, grand-father, father, and son, for they have been a succession of clowns for five generations. The most remarkable of *Joey's* predecessors was called *Jambes de fer*, from the strength and spring of his limbs : he was the grand-father and a great favourite with the ladies —*ferrum est quod amant :* he once broke a chandelier by lofty vaulting, and with a piece of the glass almost knocked out the eye of the Turkish Ambassador, who made it a formal complaint to the French Court. *Joey's* son promises much, and cannot be said to *perform* little ; for all the winter he is at Covent-Garden, and all the summer at Sadler's Wells : however, he will never be as distinguished as his father ;

"Compared with whom all other clowns are fools."

Judy. Oh, you nasty cruel brute! [Hitting him again.] I'll teach you.

Punch. But me no like such teaching. What! you're in earnest, are you?

Judy. Yes [hit], I [hit], am [hit].

Punch. I'm glad of it: me no like such jokes.* [She hits him again.] Leave off, I say. What! you won't, won't you?

Judy. No, I won't. [Hits him.]

Punch. Very well: then now come my turn to teach you. [He snatches at, and struggles with her for the stick, which he wrenches from her, and strikes her with it on the head, while she runs about to different parts of the stage to get out of his way.]

---

* This is a jest in almost every language, but it is particularly common in Italy. It is inserted in Domenichi's Collection of *Motti Burle e Facetie:* Venice, 1565. It is of a piece with the story relating to General ———, whom T. H. kicked in a ball-room. "What do you mean by that, Sir?" (cried the General). "Am I to take that as a personal affront?" — "To be sure you are," replied T. H. — "I am glad of it (returned the General), I like people to speak intelligibly — it saves the trouble of farther *explanation.*" Accordingly, T. H. heard no more from the officer; who afterwards got so often affronted, and received patiently so many insults, that he acquired the nick-name of "the *receiver* General."

How you like my teaching, Judy, my pretty dear?
[Hitting her.]

Judy. Oh, pray, Mr. Punch. No more!

Punch. Yes, one littel more lesson. [Hits her again.]
There, there, there! [She falls down with her head
over the platform of the stage; and as he continues
to hit at her, she puts up her hand to guard her head.]
Any more?

Judy. No, no, no more!　　　　[Lifting up her head.

Punch. [Knocking down her head.] I thought I
should soon make you quiet.

Judy. [Again raising her head.] No.

Punch. [Again knocking it down, and following up
his blows until she is lifeless.] Now if you're satisfied, I am. [Perceiving that she does not move.]
There, get up, Judy, my dear; I won't hit you any
more. None of your sham-Abram.* This is only
your fun. You got the head-ache? Why, you only
asleep. Get up, I say. — Well, then, get down. [Tosses
the body down with the end of his stick.] He, he,

---

* This is a very old English word; not, however, inserted
and explained by the Rev. H. J. Todd. *Sham* is said to be
derived from the Welsh, and *Abram* is from what were formerly called "Abram," or "Abraham men," who pretended
to be poor and sick, and therefore objects of charity. (See

he! [Laughing.] To lose a wife is to get a fortune.*
[Sings.]

> "Who'd be plagued with a wife
> That could set himself free
> With a rope or a knife,
> Or a good stick, like me." †

Dodsley's Old Plays, new edition, vol. ii. page 4, note 2.) To sham-Abram is a term in daily use:

> "*Sham-Abram* you may
> In any fair way,
> But you must not sham Abraham Newland."
> *T. Dibdin's Song.*

Abraham Newland is still remembered as the worthy predecessor of that most agreeable companion, Mr. Henry Hase.— The acquaintances of the latter are less numerous since the Bank of England resumed its payments in specie.

* The English proverb is, "He that loses his wife and sixpence, loses a tester." It is put into the mouth of Sancho, in Act ii. of Durfey's *Don Quixote*, Part i.

† Evidently from Juvenal, Sat. vi.

> *Ferre potes dominam salvis tot restibus ullam?*
> *Cum pateant altæ caligantesque fenestræ,*
> *Cum tibi vicinum se præbeat Æmilius pons?*

Here it seems doubtful whether the poet means to recommend the hen-pecked husband himself to use the halter, leap

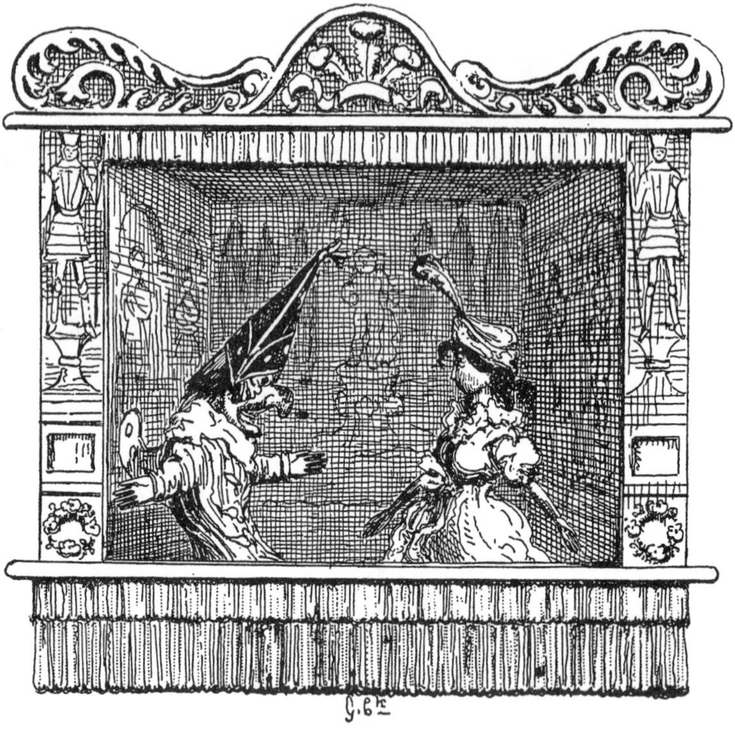
G.Ck

SCENE IV.

Enter Pretty Polly.*

Punch. [Seeing her, and singing out of *"The Beg-gar's Opera,"*† while she dances,]

> When the heart of a man is oppress'd with cares,
> The clouds are dispelled when a woman appears, &c.

Punch. [Aside.] What a beauty! What a pretty creature!‡ [Extending his arms, and then clasping

out of the window, &c., or that he should hang his wife, or give her the benefit of the air. Punch's actions supply a commentary on his words, if any were wanting.

* Sometimes called Nancy, and hence the old saying —

> "For fun and fancy,
> As Punch kissed Nancy."

† This song was probably first introduced into a puppet-show, at the time when Gay's work was so extravagantly popular; but not more popular than it deserved to be.

‡ In this copy of "Punch and Judy," Pretty Polly is merely a mute, which perhaps might recommend her to our hero, in contrast with his late spouse. In a few of the representations she speaks; and one which was popular in 1795 and 1796, contained the following scene. We ought to premise, that in that

his hands in admiration. She continues to dance, and dances round him, while he surveys her in silent delight. He then begins to sing a slow tune and foots

show, Polly was supposed to be the daughter of a gentleman whom Punch had just slain, in a quarrel regarding his performances on the sheep-bell.

ENTER POLLY, *very gaily dressed.*

Polly. Where is my father? my dear father!

Punch. [*Aside.*] What a beauty!

Polly. Who killed my poor father? Oh! Oh!   [*Cries.*

Punch. 'Twas I.

Polly. Oh! Cruel wretch, why did you kill my father?

Punch. For your sake, my love.

Polly. Oh, you barbarian!

Punch. Don't cry so, my dear. You will cry your pretty eyes out, and that would be a pity.

Polly. Oh, Oh! How could you kill him?

Punch. He would not let me have you, and so I killed him. If you take on so, I must cry too—Oh! Oh! [*Pretending to weep.*] How sorry I am!

Polly. And are you really sorry?

Punch. Yes, very sorry—look how I cry.

Polly. [*Aside.*] What a handsome young man. It is a pity he should cry so.—How the tears run down his beautiful long nose!—Did you kill my father out of love of me, and are you sorry? If you are sorry, I must forgive you.

it with her; and, as the music quickens, they jig it backwards and forwards, and sideways, to all parts of the stage. At last, Punch catches the lady in his arms and kisses her most audibly, while she appears "nothing loth." After waltzing, they dance to the tune of "*The White Cockade*," and Punch sings as follows:]

> I love you so, I love you so,
> I never will leave you; no, no, no:
> If I had all the wives of wise King Sol,
> I would kill them all for my Pretty Poll.
>
> > [*Exeunt* dancing.

ACT II.—SCENE I.

[Enter a figure dressed like a courtier, who sings a slow air, and moves to it with great gravity and solemnity. He first takes off his hat on the right of the

---

Punch. I could kill myself for love of you, much more your father.

Polly. Do you then really love me?

Punch. I do! I do!

Polly. Then I must love you!"

Then they embrace, kiss, and dance. The whole scene, barring the dancing, seems modelled upon the interview between Richard III. and Lady Anne. It is copied from the MS. we have before mentioned.

theatre, and then on the left, and carries it in his hand. He then stops in the centre; the music ceases, and suddenly his throat begins to elongate, and his head gradually rises until his neck is taller than all the rest of his body. After pausing for some time, the head sinks again; and, as soon as it has descended to its natural place, the figure *exit.**]

SCENE II.

ENTER PUNCH from behind the curtain, where he had been watching the manœuvres of the figure.

Punch. Who the devil are you, me should like to

---

* This scene is peculiar to Piccini, and he defies all the other exhibitors of puppet-shows in England to make the figure take off the hat with one hand. This is the true reason for its introduction; and it is not easy to see in what way it relates to Mr. Punch and his adventures, unless, as he is now in the midst of his career of vice and crime, the stretching of the neck is to be taken as an awful forewarning of the danger of the same kind the hero is likely to incur under the hands of Jack Ketch.

> "You have done well,
> That men must lay their murders on your neck,"

is a passage in *Othello.* — If it be meant that Punch should lay his murders on the *neck* of this mysterious personage, it is clear that there is room enough for all of them.

know, with your long neck? You may get it stretched
for you, one of these days, by somebody else.* It's
a very fine day. [Peeping out, and looking up at the
sky.] I'll go fetch my horse, and take a ride to
visit my Pretty Poll. [He sings to the tune of "*Sally
in our Alley.*"]

> Of all the girls that are so smart,
>   There's none like Pretty Polly:
> She is the darling of my heart,
>   She is so plump and jolly.

[*Exit* singing.

RE-ENTER PUNCH, leading his horse by the bridle over
his arm. It prances about, and seems very unruly.

Punch. Wo, ho! my fine fellow. Wo! ho! Hector.†

---

* "I pr'ythee keep that for the hangman." *Henry IV.*
Part I. And Punch might add, as the forewarner appears to
be a courtier, "I know thou worship'st St. Nicholas as truly
as a man of falsehood may."

† The horses of the ancient heroes of romance, especially in
Italy (the birth-place of our hero), had all their names, sometimes descriptive of their qualifications, or of peculiar marks,.
or ornaments: that of Orlando, as every body knows, was
Baiardo; that of Aglante, *Rabicano,* and that of the Cid, *Ba-*
bieca, &c. For this reason, too, Don Quixote gives his steed
the style and title of *Rozinante,* "as it was not fit that so

Stand still, can't you, and let me get my foot up to
the stirrup.

[While Punch is trying to mount, the horse runs
away round the stage, and Punch sets off after him,
catches him by the tail, and so stops him. Punch
then mounts, by sitting on the front of the stage, and
with both his hands lifting one of his legs over the
animal's back. At first, it goes pretty steadily, but
soon quickens its pace; while Punch, who does not
keep his seat very well, cries, "Wo, ho! Hector, wo,
ho!" but to no purpose, for the horse sets off at full
gallop, jerking Punch at every stride with great vio-
lence. Punch lays hold round the neck, but is ulti-
mately thrown upon the platform.*]

famous a knight's horse, and chiefly being so good a beast,
should want a known name." *Shelton's Don Quixote,* Edit.
1652, fol. 2.

* Punch is no great horseman, but it is to be remembered
that he was not a gentleman born or bred ; and, as Spenser
says,

> " But chiefly skill to ride seems a science
>   Proper to *gentle* blood."

Sir Philip Sidney opens his *Defence of Poesie* with an account of his industry at the Emperor's court in acquiring
perfection in this art, which old Ascham, in his *Schoolmaster,*

Punch. Oh, dear! Oh, Lord! Help! Help! I am murdered! I'm a dead man! Will nobody save my life? Doctor! Doctor! Come, and bring me to life again. I'm a dead man. Doctor! Doctor! Doctor!

SCENE III.

Doctor. Who calls so loud?*

Punch. Oh, dear! Oh, lord! Murder!

Doctor. What is the matter? Bless me, who is this? My good friend, Mr. Punch? Have you had an accident, or are you only taking a nap on the grass after dinner?

Punch. Oh, Doctor! Doctor! I have been thrown: I have been killed.

Doctor. No, no, Mr. Punch; not so bad as that, sir: you are not killed.

---

praises very extravagantly, quoting the "three excellent praises amongst those noble gentlemen, the old Persians — always to speak truth, to ride fair, and shoot well."

* So the Apothecary, in *Romeo and Juliet*, of whom we say, as Dante does of the she-wolf —

> *che di tutte brame*
> *Sembiava carca nella sua magrezza,*

enters at the exclamation of the hero, with "Who calls so loud?" Punch's Doctor is quite "another guess sort of a gentleman," to use a phrase of Farquhar's, "fat with full fees and no physic."

Punch. Not killed, but speechless.* Oh, Doctor! Doctor!

Doctor. Where are you hurt? Is it here? [Touching his head.]

Punch. No; lower.

Doctor. Here?   [Touching his breast.

Punch. No; lower, lower.

Doctor. Here then?   [Going downwards.

---

* A good deal has been written on the etymology and meaning of what is called an Irish *bull*, of which we have here a specimen; some have supposed it to be derived from a ridicule of the Pope's *bulls*, &c., &c.; but its origin is very simple: a *bull* is a blunder; and only let the reader pronounce the two first letters of the word *blunder*, and he immediately has the true etymology—*blunder*, or per ellipsin *bl.* Milton correctly defines a *bull*, when he says it "takes away the essence of that which it calls itself." (*Smectym, Apology.*) But rather before the time when he flourished it seems to have been almost synonimous with a jest. Thus in Shirley's "Gamester," 1637, Act iii. Hazard says to Wilding,

> ———— "He will talk desperately
> And swear he is the father of all the *bulls*
> Since Adam: if all fail, he has a project
> To print his *jests.*
>   *Wilding.* His *bulls*, you mean.
>   *Hazard.* You're right,
> And dedicate 'em to the gamesters," &c.

Punch. No ; lower still.

Doctor. Then, is your handsome leg broken ?

Punch. No ; higher. [As the Doctor leans over Punch's legs, to examine them, Punch kicks him in the eye.]

Doctor. Oh, my eye ! my eye !   [*Exit.*

Punch. [*Solus.*] Aye, you're right enough : it is my eye, and Betty Martin too.* [Jumping up and dancing and singing, tune "*Malbroug.*"]

> The Doctor is surely an ass, sirs,
> To think I'm as brittle as glass, sirs ;
> But I only fell down on the grass, sirs,
> And my hurt,—it is all my eye.

[While Punch is singing and dancing, the Doctor enters behind, and hits Punch several times on the head. Punch shakes his ears.]

Punch. Hollo ! hollo ! Doctor, what game you up to now ? Have done ! What you got there ?

---

* This joke is much more proper, in some respects, in Catholic Italy, than in Protestant England, where we have left off praying to Saints. The saying is, however, as is well known, derived from times prior to the Reformation, when *Mihi, beate Martine*, was the commencement of an address to St. Martin : the use of it, as an expression of ridicule, implying incredulity, must, of course, have been posterior to that event, when *disbelief* in the efficacy of such addresses became general.

Doctor. Physic, Mr. Punch. [Hits him.] Physic for your hurt.

Punch. Me no like physic : it give me one head-ache.

Doctor. That's because you do not take enough of it. [Hits him again.] The more you take, the more good it will do you.   [Hits him.

Punch. So you Doctors always say. Try how you like it yourself.

Doctor. We never take our own physic, if we can help it. [Hits him.] A little more, Mr. Punch, and you will soon be well. [Hits him. During this part of the dialogue, the Doctor hunts Punch to different parts of the stage, and at last gets him into a corner, and belabours him until Punch seems almost stunned.]

Punch. Oh, Doctor! Doctor! no more, no more! Enough physic for me! I am quite well now.

Doctor. Only another dose.   [Hits him.

Punch. No more! — Turn and turn about is all fair, you know. [Punch makes a desperate effort, closes with the Doctor, and after a struggle succeeds in getting the stick from him.] Now, Doctor, your turn to be physicked. [Beating the Doctor.*]

---

* We cannot call Punch *lethargicus,* but, at all events,
——— *fit pugil et medicum urget.*

Doctor. Hold, Mr. Punch! I don't want any physic, my good sir.

Punch. Oh, yes, you do; you very bad: you must take it. I the Doctor now.* [Hits him.] How do you like physic? [Hits.] It will do you good. [Hits.] This will soon cure you. [Hits.] Physic! [Hits.] Physic! [Hits.] Physic! [Hits.]

Doctor. Oh, pray, Mr. Punch, no more! One pill of that physic is a dose.

Punch. Doctors always die when they take their own physic. [Hits him.] Another small dose, and you never want physic again. [Hits him.] There; don't you feel the physic in your inside? [Punch thrusts the end of the stick into the Doctor's stomach: the Doctor falls down dead, and Punch, as before, tosses away the body with the end of his staff.] He, he, he! [Laughing.] Now, Doctor, you may cure yourself, if you can. [Sings and dances to the tune of "*Green grow the rushes, O!*"]

As one of our old translators has it,

> " He knocks down the quack
> On the flat of his back."

* " He will be the physician that should be the patient."
>   *Troilus and Cressida,* Act ii.

> Right toll de riddle doll,
> There's an end of him, by goll!*
>   I'll dance and sing,
>   Like any thing,
> With music for my Pretty Poll.   [*Exit.*

SCENE IV.

ENTER PUNCH, with a large sheep-bell, which he
rings violently, and dances about the stage, shaking
the bell and his head at the same time, and accom-
panying the music with his voice; tune "*Morgiana
in Ireland.*"

> Mr. Punch is a very gay man,
> He is the fellow the ladies for winning, oh;
> Let them do whatever they can,
> They never can stand his talking and grinning, oh.

-----

* A very respectable ancient English oath. *Goll*, in our old
writers, and in the vulgar tongue, is the same as *hand*; so that
to swear "by goll," is nothing more than to swear by one's
hand. "By goles," or "golls," is still used in the country.
Thus, in S. Rowley's *Noble Soldier*, 1634, Act iii. Baltazar
says to Onelia (a lady of Spanish and not of Irish extraction,
as might be supposed by her name), "Say'st thou me so?
Give me thy *goll*, thou art a noble girl," &c. We leave it to
future sagacious commentators on this play, to shew that
"learning is somewhere vain," and to multiply quotations on
a point never disputed.

ENTER A SERVANT, in a foreign livery.

Servant. Mr. Punch, my master, he say he no like dat noise.

Punch. [With surprise and mocking him.] Your master, he say he no like dat noise! What noise?

Servant. Dat nasty noise.

Punch. Do you call music a noise?*

Servant. My master he no lika de music, Mr. Punch, so he'll have no more noise near his house.†

---

* Our less refined ancestors used to do so. "A noise of fiddlers," "a noise of flutes," &c., are common expressions in old plays of the reigns of Elizabeth and James I. Punch's ear for music resembles that of Nick Bottom. "I have a reasonable good ear for music : let us have the tongs and the bones."

† Part of a now unacted scene in *Othello*, very much resembles this. The Clown enters, and complains of certain serenaders hired by Cassio, and tells them, "the General so likes your music, that he desires you of all loves to make no more noise with it."

1st Musician. Well, sir, we will not.

Clown. If you have any music that may not be heard, to't again : but as they say, to hear music, the General does not greatly care.

1st Musician. We have none such, sir.

Clown. Then put your pipes in your bag and hie away. Go — vanish into air ! Away !

Punch. He don't, don't he? Very well. [Punch runs about the stage ringing his bell as loudly as he can.]

Servant. Get away, I say, wid dat nasty bell.

Punch. What bell?

Servant. That bell. [Striking it with his hand.]

Punch. That's a good one. Do you call this a bell? [Patting it.] It is an organ.

Servant. I say it is a bell, a nasty bell.

Punch. I say it is an organ. [Striking him with it.] What you say it is now?

Servant. An organ, Mr. Punch.

Punch. An organ? I say it is a fiddel. Can't you see?   [Offers to strike him again.

Servant. It is a fiddel.

Punch. I say it is a drum.

Servant. It is a drum, Mr. Punch.

Punch. I say it is a trumpet.

Servant. Well, so it is a trumpet. But bell, organ, fiddel, drum, or trumpet, my master he say he no lika de music.

Punch. Then bell, organ, fiddel, drum, or trumpet, Mr. Punch he say your master is a fool.

Servant. And he say, too, he will not have it near his house.

Punch. He's a fool, I say, not to like my sweet music. Tell him so: be off. [Hits him with the bell.]

Get along. [Driving the servant round the stage, backwards, and striking him often with the bell.] Be off, be off. [Knocking him off the stage. *Exit* Servant. Punch continues to ring the bell as loudly as before, while he sings and dances.]

Re-enter Servant, slily, with a stick.

[Punch, perceiving him, retreats behind the side curtain, and remains upon the watch. The Servant does the same, but leaves the end of the stick visible. Punch again comes forward, sets down his bell very gently, and creeps across the stage (marking his steps with his hands upon the platform), to ascertain whereabouts his enemy is. He then returns to his bell, takes it up, and, going quietly over the stage, hits the Servant a heavy blow through the curtain, and *exit*, ringing his bell on the opposite side.]

Servant. You one nasty, noisy, impudent blackguard. Me catch you yet. [Hides again as before.

[Enter Punch, and strikes him as before with the bell. The Servant pops out, and aims a blow, but not quickly enough to hit Punch, who *exit*.]

Servant. You dirty scoundrel, rascal, thief, vagabond, blackguard, and liar, you shall pay for this, depend upon it.

[He stands back. Enter Punch, with his bell, who, seeing the Servant with his stick, retreats instantly, and returns, also armed with a bludgeon, which he does not at first shew. The Servant comes forward, and strikes Punch on the head so hard a blow, that it seems to confuse him.]

Servant. Me teach you how to ring you nasty, noisy bell near de gentil-men's houses.

Punch. [Recovering.] Two can play at that. [Hits the Servant with his stick. A conflict:—after a long struggle, during which the combatants exchange staves, and perform various manœuvres, Punch gains the victory, and knocks his antagonist down on the platform, by repeated blows on the head.]

Servant. Oh, dear! Oh, my head!

Punch. And oh, your tail, too. [Hitting him there.] How do you like that, and that, and that? [Hitting him each time.] Do you like that music better than the other?—This is my bell [Hits], this my organ [Hits], this my fiddel [Hits], this my drum [Hits], and this my trumpet [Hits], there! a whole concert for you.

Servant. No more! me dead.

Punch. Quite dead?

Servant. Yes, quite.

Punch. Then there's the last for luck. [Hits him

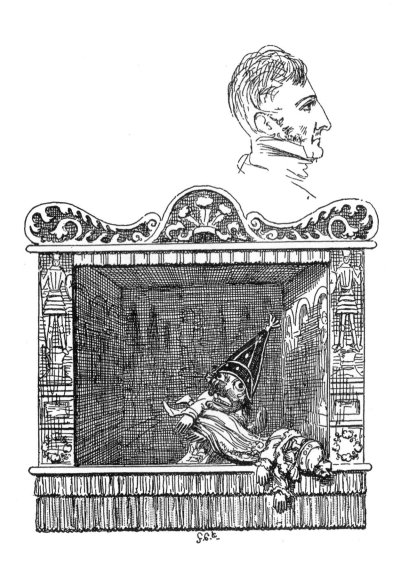

and kills him. He then takes hold of the body by its legs, swings it round two or three times, and throws it away.]

ACT III.—SCENE I.

ENTER AN OLD BLIND MAN, feeling his way with a staff. He goes to the opposite side, where he knocks.

Blind Man. Poor blind man, Mr. Punch; I hope you'll bestow your charity. I hear that you are very good and kind to the poor, Mr. Punch. Pray have pity upon me, and may you never know the loss of your tender eyes! [Listens, putting his ear to the side, and hearing nobody coming knocks again.] I lost my sight by the sands in Egypt,* poor blind man. Pray, Mr. Punch, have compassion upon the poor stone blind. [Coughs and spits over the side.] Only a halfpenny to buy something for my bad cough. Only one halfpenny. [Knocks again.]

---

* Of course, this explanation of the cause of blindness was inserted after Sir R. Abercrombie's expedition to Egypt, when many beggars were seen about the streets asking alms on the same score. Before that date, some other popular cause was, no doubt, assigned.

ENTER PUNCH, and receives one of the knocks, intended for the door, upon his head.

Punch. Hollo! you old blind blackguard, can't you see?

Blind Man. No, Mr. Punch. Pray, sir, bestow your charity upon a poor blind man, with a bad cough. [Coughs.]

Punch. Get along, get along; don't trouble me:— nothing for you.

Blind Man. Only a halfpenny! Oh, dear! my cough is so bad! [Coughs, and spits in Punch's face.

Punch. Hollo! Was my face the dirtiest place you could find to spit in?* Get away! you nasty old blackguard! Get away! [Seizes the blind man's staff, and knocks him off the stage.—Punch hums a tune, and dances to it; and then begins to sing, in the mock Italian style, the following words, pretending to play the fiddle on his arm, with the stick.]

---

* This joke is of Italian origin. Bandello (Part iii. Nov. 42.) makes the Spanish Ambassador spit in the face of one of the servants of the famous Roman courtezan Imperia, whose house was most splendidly furnished. It is, however, older than Bandello's time; and it is also found in the Italian jest book, before quoted, collected by Domenichi in 1565.

When I think on you, my jewel,*
    Wonder not my heart is sad;
You're so fair, and yet so cruel,
    You're enough to drive me mad.

On thy lover take some pity:
    And relieve his bitter smart.
Think you Heaven has made you pretty,
    But to break your lover's heart?

SCENE II

ENTER A CONSTABLE.

Constable. Leave off your singing, Mr. Punch, for I'm come to make you sing on the wrong side of your mouth.

Punch. Why, who the devil are you?

Constable. Don't you know me?

Punch. No, and don't want to know you.

Constable. Oh, but you must: I am the constable.

Punch. And who sent for you?

Constable. I'm sent for you.

* A real Italian air and song, introduced by Piccini, of which this is a translation: the first words of the original are—
    Quando pens' io à la mia bella.

Punch. I don't want constable. I can settle my own business without constable, I thank you. I don't want constable.

Constable. But the constable wants you.

Punch. The devil he does! What for, pray?

Constable. You killed Mr. Scaramouch. You knocked his head off his shoulders.

Punch. What's that to you? If you stay here much longer, I'll serve you the same.

Constable. Don't tell me. You have committed murder, and I've a warrant for you.

Punch. And I've a warrant for you. [Punch knocks him down, and dances and sings about the stage to the tune of *"Green grow the rushes, O!"*]

ENTER AN OFFICER, in a cocked hat with a cockade, and a long pigtail.*

Officer. Stop your noise, my fine fellow.

Punch. Shan't.

Officer. I'm an officer.

Punch. Very well. Did I say you were not?

* The ordinary performers of puppet-shows do not seem clearly to understand the distinction between an officer of the army and an officer of the police.

Officer. You must go with me. You killed your wife and child.

Punch. They were my own, I suppose; and I had a right to do what I liked with them.

Officer. We shall see that, I'm come to take you up.

Punch. And I'm come to take you down. [Punch knocks him down, and sings and dances as before.]

ENTER JACK KETCH, in a fur-cap. Punch, while dancing, runs up against him without seeing him.

Punch. [With some symptoms of alarm.] My dear Sir,—I beg you one thousand pardon: very sorry.

J. Ketch. Aye, you'll be sorry enough before I've done with you. Don't you know me?

Punch. Oh, sir, I know you very well, and I hope you very well, and Mrs. Ketch very well.

J. Ketch. Mr. Punch, you're a very bad man. Why did you kill the Doctor?

Punch. In self-defence.

J. Ketch. That won't do.

Punch. He wanted to kill me.

J. Ketch. How?

Punch. With his d——d physic.

J. Ketch. That's all gammon. You must come to prison: my name's Ketch.

Punch. Ketch that then. [Punch knocks down Jack Ketch, and continues to dance and sing.*]

[Enter behind, one after the other, the Constable, the Officer, and Jack Ketch. They fall upon Punch in the order in which they enter, and, after a noisy struggle, they pin him in a corner, and finally carry him off, while he lustily calls out "Help! murder!" &c.

SCENE III.

The curtain at the back of the stage rises, and dis-

---

* After the defeat of Jack Ketch, we have sometimes seen, with a total disregard of his rank and office, the Chief Justice of England introduced, for the purpose of making the caption of Punch. The dialogue between the two was equally *infra dignitatem*, at least on the part of the first Judge of the land.

Chief Justice. Hollo! Punch, my boy!

Punch. Hollo! who are you with your head like a cauliflower?

Ch. Just. Don't you know me? I'm the Lord Chief Justice.

Punch. I don't care if you're the Lord Chancellor. You shan't get me into Chancery, that's all.

Ch. Just. But I shall get you into prison. — You're a murderer! you've killed I don't know how many people.

Punch. If you don't know, you had better go and learn.

Ch. Just. That won't do, my fine fellow. You're a murderer, and you must come and be hanged.

Punch. I'll be hanged if I do. [Knocks down the Chief Justice, and dances and sings.]

covers Punch in prison, rubbing his nose against the bars and poking it through them.

Punch. Oh, dear! Oh, dear! what will become of poor pill-garlick now. My Pretty Poll, when shall I see you again? [Sings to the air of *"Water parted from the sea."*]

> Punch, when parted from his dear,
>   Still must sing in doleful tune.
> I wish I had those rascals here,
>   I'd settle all their hashes soon!

ENTER JACK KETCH. He fixes a gibbet on the platform of the stage, and *exit.*

Punch. Well, I declare now, that very pretty! That must be a gardener. What a handsome tree he has planted just opposite the window, for a prospect!*

ENTER THE CONSTABLE. He places a ladder against the gibbet, and *exit.*

Punch. Stop thief! stop thief! There's one pretty rascal for you. He come back again and get up the ladder to steal the fruit out of the tree.

---

* Of course Punch does not think what he says, but he only "plays with his fate:" as Racine remarks in *Athalie* (Act ii.),
    Les malheurs n'avoient pas abattu sa fierté,
although in the commencement of this scene the recollection of his mistress had a little " rebated the edge of his hilarity."

ENTER TWO MEN with a coffin. They set it down on
the platform, and *exeunt.*

Punch. What that for, I wonder? Oh, dear, I see
now: what one fool I was! That is a large basket for
the fruit be put into.

RE-ENTER JACK KETCH.

J. Ketch. Now, Mr. Punch, you may come out, if
you like it.

Punch. Thank you, kindly; but me very well where
I am. This very nice place, and pretty prospect.

J. Ketch. What, won't you come out, and have a
good dinner for nothing?

Punch. Much obliged, Mr. Ketch, but I have had
my dinner for nothing already.*

J. Ketch. Then a good supper?

---

* Among the *Rime burlesche di varj Autori,* originally collected by Grazzini, is a very humorous *Capitolo,* in praise of
debt (attributed by some to Berni, and by the editor of Tas-
soni's *Secchia Rapita,* Venice, 1747, to Orazio Toscanella),
with some lines quite in the spirit in which our hero speaks in
the text.

> *Non so più bello star, ch'entro d'un muro, &c.*

> A prison, truly, is a charming place,
>> Where all the livelong day we may be idle;
> A blest retreat where mind has double space,
>> Because our bodies we are forc'd to bridle:

Punch. I never eat suppers: they are not wholesome.

J. Ketch. But you must come out. Come out and be hanged.*

Punch. You would not be so cruel.

J. Ketch. Why were you so cruel as to commit so many murders?

Punch. But that's no reason why you should be cruel, too, and murder me.†

J. Ketch. Come, directly.

Punch. I can't; I got one bone in my leg.

J. Ketch. And you've got one bone in your neck, but that shall be soon broken.—Then I must fetch you. [He goes to the prison, and after a struggle, in which Punch calls out, "Mercy! mercy! I'll never do so again!" Jack Ketch brings him out to the front of the stage.]

Where all that we require is *given,* not *bought,*
　　I mean all good things, and are but denied ill.
When to this happy rest we once are brought,
　　It verifies the words of Aristotle—
Gross sense decays, and we have time for thought.

* A direct plagiarism from Shakspeare : "Master Barnardine, you must rise and be hanged." *Measure for Measure.*

† An instance how Punch's self-possession never forsakes him. In a single sentence he confutes all who contend that man by law should have power over the life of his fellow man.

Punch. Oh, dear! Oh, dear! Be quiet—can't you let me be?

J. Ketch. Now, Mr. Punch, no more delay. Put your head through this loop.

Punch. Through there! What for?

J. Ketch. Aye, through there.

Punch. What for?—I don't know how.

J. Ketch. It is very easy: only put your head through here.

Punch. What, so? [Poking his head on one side of the noose.]

J. Ketch. No, no, here!

Punch. So, then? [Poking his head on the other side.]

J. Ketch. Not so, you fool.

Punch. Mind, how you call fool: try if you can do it yourself. Only shew me how, and I do it directly.

J. Ketch. Very well; I will. There, you see my head, and you see this loop: put it in, so. [Putting his head through the noose.]

Punch. And pull it tight, so! [He pulls the body forcibly down, and hangs Jack Ketch.] Huzza! Huzza! [Punch takes down the corpse, and places it in the coffin: he then stands back. Enter two, who remove the gibbet, and placing the coffin upon it, dance with it on their shoulders grotesquely, and *exeunt.*]

Punch. There they go. They think they have got Mr. Punch safe enough. [Sings.]

> They're out! they're out! I've done the trick!
> Jack Ketch is dead—I'm free;
> I do not care, now, if Old Nick
> Himself should come for me.

[*Exit.*

SCENE IV.

ENTER PUNCH with a stick. He dances about, beating time on the front of the stage, and singing to the tune of "*Green grow the rushes, O!*"

> Right foll de riddle loll
> I'm the boy to do 'em all.
> Here's a stick
> To thump Old Nick,
> If he by chance upon me call.

ENTER THE DEVIL. He just peeps in at the corner of the stage, and *exit.*

Punch. [Much frightened, and retreating as far as he can.] Oh, dear! Oh, Lord! Talk of the devil, and he pop up his horns. There the old gentleman is, sure enough. [A pause and dead silence, while Punch continues to gaze at the spot where the Devil appeared. The Devil comes forward.] Good, kind Mr. Devil, I never did you any harm, but all the good in my power.

—There, don't come any nearer. How you do, Sir?
[Collecting courage.] I hope you and all your respectable family well? Much obliged for this visit—Good
morning—should be sorry to keep you, for I know
you have a great deal of business when you come
to London. [The Devil advances.] Oh, dear! What
will become of me? [The Devil darts at Punch, who
escapes, and aims a blow at his enemy: the Devil
eludes it, as well as many others, laying his head on
the platform, and slipping it rapidly backwards and
forwards, so that Punch, instead of striking him, only
repeatedly hits the boards.]   [*Exit* Devil.

Punch. He, he, he! [Laughing.] He's off: he knew
which side his bread butter'd on. He one deep,
cunning devil. [Punch is alarmed by hearing a strange
supernatural whirring noise, something like the rapid
motion of fifty spinning-wheels, and again retreats to
the corner, fearfully waiting the event.]

RE-ENTER THE DEVIL, with a stick. [He makes up
    to Punch, who retreats round the back of the stage,
    and they stand eyeing one another and fencing at
    opposite sides. At last, the Devil makes a blow at
    Punch, which tells on the back of his head.]

Punch. Oh, my head! What is that for? Pray, Mr.
Devil, let us be friends. [The Devil hits him again,

and Punch begins to take it in dudgeon, and to grow angry.] Why, you must be one very stupid Devil not to know your best friend when you see him. [The Devil hits him again.] Be quiet, I say, you hurt me! Well, if you won't, we must try which is best man, — Punch or the Devil.

[Here commences a terrific combat between the Devil and Punch: in the beginning, the latter has much the worst of it, being hit by his black adversary when and where he pleases. At last, the Devil seems to grow weary, and Punch succeeds in planting several heavy blows. The balance being restored, the fight is kept up for some time, and towards the conclusion Punch has the decided advantage, and drives his enemy before him. The Devil is stunned by repeated blows on the head and horns, and falls forward on the platform, where Punch completes his victory, and knocks the breath out of his body. Punch then puts his staff up the Devil's black clothes, and whirls him round in the air, exclaiming, "Huzza! huzza! the Devil's dead!"]

The Curtain falls.

FINIS.

BIBLIOGRAPHICAL NOTE.

BIBLIOGRAPHICAL NOTE.

GEORGE CRUIKSHANK was born in London, September 27, 1792. His father, Isaac Cruikshank, was an artist of indifferent ability who, however, had at one time or another exhibited paintings on the walls of the Royal Academy, and young George, therefore, was, in his earliest years, subject to the influences which were destined to shape his career along much the same line as his father's. Starting as an apprentice, the boy's first training came in etching the backgrounds of some of his father's plates, and so rapidly did he progress from this hack work that, by the time of the elder Cruikshank's death, George, though still in his teens, was already known as a popular artist of the day. Even in this early work he clearly revealed a technical skill as an etcher which, in the opinion of many competent judges, ranks Cruikshank among the foremost in this field, while he also disclosed, as a supplement to his genius, an understanding of human nature, a delicacy of feeling, and a remarkable insight into character, qualities so necessary to a truly great illustrator and cartoonist.

Cruikshank was fortunate indeed to have lived in a period so rich in material for his work, and his subjects cover a field whose limits seem to have been determined only by the requirements of the publishers themselves. Albert Cohen, in his recent bibliography, lists 863 items among illustrated books alone, to say nothing of the numerous caricatures and theatrical and political broadsides. Among the books that Cruikshank illustrated are to be found the works of Dickens, Thackeray, Scott, Ainsworth, and Mrs. Ewing, while the political broadsides include his gallant support of the unfortunate Queen Caroline and attacks upon King George IV, who was for years the victim of the artist's satire and ridicule.

In 1828, at the height of his career, Cruikshank was commissioned by Prowett, the publisher, to execute the plates for Punch and Judy. It was a particularly happy selection, for both the pathos and humour of the puppet-show appealed to his imagination and were so successfully delineated that very few copies of the first edition have survived the century since publication. The book was literally read to pieces. The original drawings coloured by the artist himself were presented by the late Mrs. Cruikshank to the National Arts Library in the South Kensington Museum, London, where they may be seen to-day.

The first edition, published by S. Prowett, London, 1828, was issued plain and coloured in greenish paper boards, with label on back. There are twenty-four etchings (including frontispiece which is not numbered) and four woodcuts designed and etched by George Cruikshank. These illustrations are accompanied by the dialogue of the puppet-show by John Payne Collier, who also wrote an account of the origin of the show and of puppet-plays in England, which is also included in the volume. The coloured plates in the first edition should be upon stiff, Whatman paper of vellum texture. The illustrations were also issued without letterpress in the same year. The cleverly written dialogue was taken down by Collier at the same time that Cruikshank made his drawings. As librarian to the Duke of Devonshire, Collier had access to the chief collections of early English literature throughout the Kingdom, and although to-day he is probably best known for

his Shaksperean forgeries, he compiled valuable bibliographical and critical accounts of many of the rarest books in the
English language. He was also a dramatic critic of note, edited
collections of early dramas, and reprinted many tracts of extreme rarity, some for the Percy and Camden Societies.

It was characteristic of Cruikshank that he often etched
portraits, notes, or amusing sketches on the margin of his
plates and one of the most delightful of these, a delicately
etched profile of himself as a young man, appears on the bor-
der of the plate facing page 127 of this series. This likeness
did not go down to posterity in the book, however, for the
portrait was erased after only six proofs had been pulled.

The English version of Punch and Judy as we know it to-
day was first pictured by Cruikshank, who reproduced the
costumes of the puppets as he had seen them in the show
given by Piccini, the Italian Puppetman. There are an unbe-
lievable number of periods represented in the style of dress,
beginning with Punch, whose much-discussed costume of red
and yellow is rather obscure in origin, and continuing on to
the modernly clothed Doctor and Beadle. The clown and the
dog Toby are Elizabethan, for Toby wears a ruff of that period
and the clown is in doublet and hose. Judy is truly Georgian
in her mob-cap, apron, and bed-jacket, while the baby wears
long clothes, as all proper babies should, the hangman is in
orthodox black, the ghost wears a respectable shroud, and the
Devil appears with his inevitable horns. It is interesting to
note that much of Punch and Judy is of an allegorical nature,
and in the closing scenes we find Punch triumphing over
evil and overcoming ennui in the shape of the Dog, defeating

disease in the guise of the Doctor, outwitting the Devil himself, and beating Death to death.

Since the Sixteenth Century the show seems to have been a familiar sight and we hear of it from diarists, poets, novelists, satirists, and historians. Pepys, in his diary, tells us in a characteristic entry under August 16, 1666, that "I with my wife . . . by coach to Moorfields and there saw Polinchinello which pleases me mightily." Steele makes reference in the *Tatler* to the dancing of Punch and his wife, Swift writes of the hero in a Dialogue between Mad Mullinix and Timothy, while Fielding in *Tom Jones* complains that "the fine and serious part of the provoked husband had been included in a Punch show seen by Tom Jones." Perhaps more amusing than any was a representation of Nelson, after the battle of the Nile, trying to persuade Punch, in an animated dialogue, to come aboard his ship and help him fight the French.

But it remained for Thackeray, whose own ability as an illustrator was by no means small, to make a most eloquent tribute to Cruikshank's genius. He says : "Week by week for thirty years to produce something new ; some smiling offspring of painful labor, quite independent and distinct from its ten thousand jovial brethren. . . . He has told a thousand truths in as many strange and fascinating ways ; he has given a thousand new and pleasant thoughts to millions of people ; he has never used his wit dishonestly. How little do we think of the extraordinary power of this man, and how ungrateful we are to him ! It is, indeed, no trifle to be a good caricaturist."

ANNE LYON HAIGHT

New York, July 9, 1929

A CATALOG OF SELECTED
DOVER BOOKS
IN ALL FIELDS OF INTEREST

A CATALOG OF SELECTED DOVER
BOOKS IN ALL FIELDS OF INTEREST

CONCERNING THE SPIRITUAL IN ART, Wassily Kandinsky. Pioneering work by father of abstract art. Thoughts on color theory, nature of art. Analysis of earlier masters. 12 illustrations. 80pp. of text. 5⅜ x 8½.   0-486-23411-8

CELTIC ART: The Methods of Construction, George Bain. Simple geometric techniques for making Celtic interlacements, spirals, Kells-type initials, animals, humans, etc. Over 500 illustrations. 160pp. 9 x 12. (Available in U.S. only.)   0-486-22923-8

AN ATLAS OF ANATOMY FOR ARTISTS, Fritz Schider. Most thorough reference work on art anatomy in the world. Hundreds of illustrations, including selections from works by Vesalius, Leonardo, Goya, Ingres, Michelangelo, others. 593 illustrations. 192pp. 7⅛ x 10¼.   0-486-20241-0

CELTIC HAND STROKE-BY-STROKE (Irish Half-Uncial from "The Book of Kells"): An Arthur Baker Calligraphy Manual, Arthur Baker. Complete guide to creating each letter of the alphabet in distinctive Celtic manner. Covers hand position, strokes, pens, inks, paper, more. Illustrated. 48pp. 8¼ x 11.   0-486-24336-2

EASY ORIGAMI, John Montroll. Charming collection of 32 projects (hat, cup, pelican, piano, swan, many more) specially designed for the novice origami hobbyist. Clearly illustrated easy-to-follow instructions insure that even beginning papercrafters will achieve successful results. 48pp. 8¼ x 11.   0-486-27298-2

BLOOMINGDALE'S ILLUSTRATED 1886 CATALOG: Fashions, Dry Goods and Housewares, Bloomingdale Brothers. Famed merchants' extremely rare catalog depicting about 1,700 products: clothing, housewares, firearms, dry goods, jewelry, more. Invaluable for dating, identifying vintage items. Also, copyright-free graphics for artists, designers. Co-published with Henry Ford Museum & Greenfield Village. 160pp. 8¼ x 11.   0-486-25780-0

THE ART OF WORLDLY WISDOM, Baltasar Gracian. "Think with the few and speak with the many," "Friends are a second existence," and "Be able to forget" are among this 1637 volume's 300 pithy maxims. A perfect source of mental and spiritual refreshment, it can be opened at random and appreciated either in brief or at length. 128pp. 5⅜ x 8½.   0-486-44034-6

JOHNSON'S DICTIONARY: A Modern Selection, Samuel Johnson (E. L. McAdam and George Milne, eds.). This modern version reduces the original 1755 edition's 2,300 pages of definitions and literary examples to a more manageable length, retaining the verbal pleasure and historical curiosity of the original. 480pp. 5⁵⁄₁₆ x 8¼.   0-486-44089-3

ADVENTURES OF HUCKLEBERRY FINN, Mark Twain, Illustrated by E. W. Kemble. A work of eternal richness and complexity, a source of ongoing critical debate, and a literary landmark, Twain's 1885 masterpiece about a barefoot boy's journey of self-discovery has enthralled readers around the world. This handsome clothbound reproduction of the first edition features all 174 of the original black-and-white illustrations. 368pp. 5⅜ x 8½.   0-486-44322-1

CATALOG OF DOVER BOOKS

LIGHT AND SHADE: A Classic Approach to Three-Dimensional Drawing, Mrs. Mary P. Merrifield. Handy reference clearly demonstrates principles of light and shade by revealing effects of common daylight, sunshine, and candle or artificial light on geometrical solids. 13 plates. 64pp. 5⅜ x 8½. 0-486-44143-1

ASTROLOGY AND ASTRONOMY: A Pictorial Archive of Signs and Symbols, Ernst and Johanna Lehner. Treasure trove of stories, lore, and myth, accompanied by more than 300 rare illustrations of planets, the Milky Way, signs of the zodiac, comets, meteors, and other astronomical phenomena. 192pp. 8⅜ x 11.

0-486-43981-X

JEWELRY MAKING: Techniques for Metal, Tim McCreight. Easy-to-follow instructions and carefully executed illustrations describe tools and techniques, use of gems and enamels, wire inlay, casting, and other topics. 72 line illustrations and diagrams. 176pp. 8¼ x 10⅞. 0-486-44043-5

MAKING BIRDHOUSES: Easy and Advanced Projects, Gladstone Califf. Easy-to-follow instructions include diagrams for everything from a one-room house for bluebirds to a forty-two-room structure for purple martins. 56 plates; 4 figures. 80pp. 8¾ x 6⅝. 0-486-44183-0

LITTLE BOOK OF LOG CABINS: How to Build and Furnish Them, William S. Wicks. Handy how-to manual, with instructions and illustrations for building cabins in the Adirondack style, fireplaces, stairways, furniture, beamed ceilings, and more. 102 line drawings. 96pp. 8¾ x 6⅝. 0-486-44259-4

THE SEASONS OF AMERICA PAST, Eric Sloane. From "sugaring time" and strawberry picking to Indian summer and fall harvest, a whole year's activities described in charming prose and enhanced with 79 of the author's own illustrations. 160pp. 8¼ x 11. 0-486-44220-9

THE METROPOLIS OF TOMORROW, Hugh Ferriss. Generous, prophetic vision of the metropolis of the future, as perceived in 1929. Powerful illustrations of towering structures, wide avenues, and rooftop parks—all features in many of today's modern cities. 59 illustrations. 144pp. 8¼ x 11. 0-486-43727-2

THE PATH TO ROME, Hilaire Belloc. This 1902 memoir abounds in lively vignettes from a vanished time, recounting a pilgrimage on foot across the Alps and Apennines in order to "see all Europe which the Christian Faith has saved." 77 of the author's original line drawings complement his sparkling prose. 272pp. 5⅜ x 8½.

0-486-44001-X

THE HISTORY OF RASSELAS: Prince of Abissinia, Samuel Johnson. Distinguished English writer attacks eighteenth-century optimism and man's unrealistic estimates of what life has to offer. 112pp. 5⅜ x 8½. 0-486-44094-X

A VOYAGE TO ARCTURUS, David Lindsay. A brilliant flight of pure fancy, where wild creatures crowd the fantastic landscape and demented torturers dominate victims with their bizarre mental powers. 272pp. 5⅜ x 8½. 0-486-44198-9

Paperbound unless otherwise indicated. Available at your book dealer, online at **www.doverpublications.com**, or by writing to Dept. GI, Dover Publications, Inc., 31 East 2nd Street, Mineola, NY 11501. For current price information or for free catalogs (please indicate field of interest), write to Dover Publications or log on to **www.doverpublications.com** and see every Dover book in print. Dover publishes more than 500 books each year on science, elementary and advanced mathematics, biology, music, art, literary history, social sciences, and other areas.